Where the States Stand on Civil Rights

WHERE THE STATES STAND ON CIVIL RIGHTS

BY *Richard Barnett* AND *Joseph Garai*

 INC.

New York

Distributed by Sterling Publishing Co., Inc., New York

CONTENTS

INTRODUCTION

"In a way, the Negro college students are seeking to save what has been so precious about our America and what bids fair to be lost; our love of individual liberty and our readiness to fight for it in the face of the grossest manifestations of tyranny, in the teeth of massive state power."

A SPEECH BY ROY WILKINS,
EXECUTIVE SECRETARY OF THE NAACP

It is the purpose of this book to document the actual condition of civil rights in each of the fifty states. This ambitious task has never before been attempted because it has been, manifestly, impossible. The civil rights reality changes in America, day by day, hour by hour, in a hundred particulars. Laws are passed—by the Congress, state legislatures, and even city councils, that somewhere, somehow, change the reality of the previous day. These are at least recorded. Many even greater transformations that are achieved by the private agencies in the field or by voluntary citizens' groups, pass without comment. It is often only when a Jew becomes governor of a state, or an Irish-Catholic President of the United States, that Americans realize how their attitudes to minority groups have changed.

There are two answers as to why such an ambitious compilation as *Where the States Stand on Civil Rights* has been undertaken now. The most basic impetus is that simple wonder and disquiet most Americans feel when they read about "Freedom Rides" and "sit-ins." What is the extent of the deprivation, discrimination and segregation we Americans practice against 20% of our fellow citizens? Is there any way that white Americans can conceivably feel what it is to be a Negro in the United States in 1961? How many of us, for instance, who do not vote would feel differently if we could not vote?

A passionate belief in education is shared by all Americans; would most of us have the determination of the southern Negroes to get it? How does it feel to be unable to buy a decent home for your family, as is the case with most northern Negroes? It is to at least venture a documentary background for questions like this that *Where the States Stand on Civil Rights* has been written.

The other reason for writing this book at this time is much simpler. Sufficient information is now available. For a number of years several dedicated research organizations, such as the Anti-Defamation League of B'nai Brith, The American Jewish Committee and the Southern School Reporting Service, have been compiling invaluable reports and studies in every area of civil rights. The national action organizations, such as The National Association for the Advancement of Colored People (NAACP), The Congress of Racial Equality (CORE), The Urban League and The Southern Christian Leadership Conference (SCLC), have all found time, despite busy programs, to publish countless articles and annual reports. Each of these organizations have made important contributions to the development of civil rights in the United States. Any assessment of the relative weight of these contributions is not included in the purpose of this book.

But more important than any of these individual sources as a research factor was the organization of the United States Commission on Civil Rights in 1957 as an independent agency within the Executive Branch of the federal government. The subsequent formation by the Commission of Advisory Committees in every state in the union made available for the first time (in the words of the then Majority Leader, Lyndon Johnson), "a useful instrument that can gather facts instead of charges; that can sift out the truth from the fancies; and can return with recommendations which will be of assistance to all reasonable men." Citizens of each state in the Union were now obliged to conscientiously examine and report on civil rights conditions in their state. These reports and the other findings of the commission have served as an invaluable basis for this book.

It is the total intention of *Where the States Stand on Civil Rights* to clarify the civil rights situation of each of the minority groups in each of the states. But as undoubtedly the most significant aspect of the American civil rights story in the last ten years has been the efforts of the country's oldest minority group, the Negroes, to achieve the full rights of citizenship, their condition is emphasized.

Several reasons have been advanced for the recent upsurge in Negro agitation for civil rights, a few of them distinctly uncomplimentary to Americans. One view holds that the increased opportunity that the Negroes received during the Roosevelt Administrations whetted the determination of these minority citizens to receive the complete prerogatives of the majority. The opinion of James Baldwin, Lorraine Hansberry and other prominent Negro intellectuals is that the upsurge is itself illusory. They maintain that there always has been deep Negro dissatisfaction and strong Negro protest about the state of Negro civil rights in America but that now outside forces have compelled the white community to face the problem as urgent. The emergence of countless African states is one reason, they feel, that has brought the United States to the recognition of the Negro petition. In any case, it is not the intention of this book to attempt to define or describe the "new" Negro. It is the purpose to document, among other facets of the civil rights story, what he has done.

A word of caution must be added about the comprehensiveness of the book. Space simply does not permit full documentation of each and every discriminatory practice in every state. Many of the instances quoted for one state could apply equally forcefully to another. An excellent illustration of this editorial policy is the accounting of barbershop discrimination in Iowa. It happens that there is unassailable documentation of this practice in that state. Negroes know, however, that their chances of getting a haircut in a white barbershop are no better in most of the other states.

In every state the most significant patterns have been described. This format, after some thought, has been adopted deliberately. *Where the States Stand on Civil Rights* has been written in the frank hope that it will reach the largest possible readership. It is not for the experts in the field; they already know the facts. It is not a collection of case studies but an over-all appraisal that, it is hoped, will be read as a modern journey through America. For these reasons it must always be borne in mind that there are many constant discriminatory realities that are not even commented upon within these covers. You know many of them. Negroes, Jews, and many other minority groups are not welcome at the majority of country clubs. A large number of fraternities and sororities still "blackball" minority groups. Most American churches, both in the North and the South, are still totally segregated. Every American can add significantly to this brief list. They are not reported in *Where the States Stand on Civil Rights* not only because there is no authoritative catalogue of such discrimination but because the state-by-state repetition of such well-known examples would rapidly become more depressing than enlightening.

Where the States Stand on Civil Rights presumes to be up-to-date, through personal or published sources, as of August of 1961. In several key instances events through September of 1961 have been included.

A short note to foreign readers may be appropriate in conclusion. It is the sincere hope of the authors that this compilation, with both its good and its bad, will find its way into the hands of such readers. But it must be pointed out that Montgomery, Alabama, is not Sharpesville, South Africa. Federal marshals flew into Montgomery with the full power of the U.S. Government to protect the protesting "Freedom Riders." America has a long history of grievously mistreating many of its minority citizens but no codified "apartheid," even in the Deep South, has ever existed in this country since the Civil War. Martin Luther King may have been arrested on a dubious traffic charge in Georgia but he attracted such national support within a few hours that the charge was dropped.

In the words of Attorney General Robert Kennedy, in answer to an African reporter: "Yes, grave problems exist, but the most important thing is that the U.S. Government and the vast majority of the people are trying to do something about it. We are making progress. But, monsieur, we will continue to have problems."

It is the "grave" civil rights problems in every state of the Union, both North and South, that this book attempts to document; it is to the "vast majority" of the American people who might care to do something about it, that this book is addressed.

September, 1961, New York, N. Y.   RICHARD BARNETT

ALABAMA

"I'm a segregationist, and I tell you 98% of the people down here feel the way I do. There shouldn't be any battles over rights. There shouldn't even be court fights. We have to give the colored people pride in themselves and pride in their communities. A fellow who's making money, he doesn't worry about things like riding buses."

GOVERNOR JOHN PATTERSON OF ALABAMA

Alabama, alphabetically the first state in the Union, was also the first state in the news of civil rights during 1961. On May 14, a Greyhound bus carrying a mixed group of Negroes and whites was ambushed and set afire outside of Anniston, Alabama, 100 miles north of the state capital of Montgomery. On the same day another group of integrated riders were set upon and beaten by a white mob when they attempted to enter segregated terminal facilities in the Trailways bus station in Birmingham.

Both of the buses were carrying members of the Congress of Racial Equality on trips planned to test segregated transportation facilities in the Deep South; within a few hours their name "Freedom Riders" was known throughout the country; within a few days headlines and pictures of the burning bus and pipe-swinging mobs had flashed around the world—severely damaging United States prestige abroad and bringing Alabama to the state of martial law.

VOTING

The entrance of the federal government, through the Justice Department, into the Tuskegee, Ala., gerrymandering dispute has again highlighted the difficulty of Negroes in securing their voting rights in Alabama. Discrimination in voting is reported in several areas of Alabama but the Tuskegee struggle has been the most bitter and will undoubtedly continue to be so as it enters its most critical phase.

Tuskegee, home of the famous Negro university, Tuskegee Institute, is a market center for a large surrounding agricultural region. Since the end of World War II, the local Negroes have been pressing for voting registration rights and despite every harassment and discouragement by local white officials, appeared to be succeeding in achieving a large Negro registration. This posed a major crisis for local and county officials, for as soon as the Negroes attained registration even roughly commensurate with their population proportion, the structure of political power in the area would be radically altered. The reaction of the white community was consequently radical.

A bill was introduced in the state legislature to redraw the city limits of Tuskegee from a square to a 26-sided gerrymand object which removed 97.5% of the registered Negro voters. Two weeks later the Negro community responded by initiating a boycott of the local white merchants. The state legislature responded in turn by abolishing Macon County (of which Tuskegee was the largest part) and attaching parts of the dismembered whole to five adjoining counties where Macon's growing registration would be dispersed and impotent.

The conflict has grown progressively more bitter. Innumerable businesses have closed; the controversy has been thoroughly ventilated in hearings before the United States Commission on Civil Rights and other arenas; suits and counter-suits have been fought up through the courts and the enmity between the two communities has hardened.

In September, 1961, the U.S. Supreme Court ruled that the gerrymandering legislation was null and void.

EDUCATION

Alabama is one of the few states that has made absolutely no progress toward desegregation of its school districts since the 1954 Supreme Court decision. The state has circumvented that decision in a number of ways. A pupil placement law, in operation since 1955, has been held by the Supreme Court (in 1958) to be not unconstitutional on its face. The court had to presume that the law would be administered without regard to race or color. New cases, involving alleged discrimination, are now being prepared for the courts. Alabama also has given each child, through its parent, the right to choose whether or not to attend a school provided for members of its own race. This legal maneuver is designed to remove the responsibility for maintaining segregation from the state to the citizen— making the practice, therefore, even more invulnerable to change.

Ever since the inconclusive termination of the Autherine Lucy case, which wound its way through the University of Alabama campus and the courts of the land for seven years, the University has been under court order to admit qualified Negro students. It has not done so to date and neither has any other state institution of higher learning in Alabama. At the height of the sit-in demonstrations that swept the South in the spring of 1960, a number of students were expelled from Alabama State College, the Negro institution for higher learning in Alabama, for their protest activities. These acts were upheld by state courts.

EMPLOYMENT

There is a great degree of employment discrimination in Alabama, as in most states of the Deep South. By and large, Negroes are limited to unskilled jobs except in cases where they serve their own community. The recent racial tension in the state is certain to have adverse economic effects on both Negro and white workers. The *Wall Street Journal* has estimated that Alabama's rapid industrial expansion will inevitably decline as a result of the recent strife. A top official of one of Birmingham's largest banks was quoted: "We've been hurt and hurt bad. In the last few days, I bet I've spent more than $50 in telephone calls trying to convince a big Ohio company that it should locate in Alabama. But I'm afraid we've lost it . . . and lost it strictly because of the unrest down here."

HOUSING

Negro housing in Alabama is segregated, substandard and overage.

PUBLIC ACCOMMODATIONS

Ever since the Reverend Martin Luther King and the Montgomery Improvement Association organized the famous and successful Montgomery bus boycott several years ago, various aspects of public accommodations in Alabama have been the object of Negro impatience with discrimination and segregation. Reverend King's Southern Christian Leadership Conference, a regional organization of prominent Negro religious leaders, has been active in many Alabama communities pressing for liberalization of the state's segregation traditions.

Before the arrival of the "Freedom Riders" in Anniston, the most dramatic protest of Alabama Negroes against the state's segregated public accommodations was the rash of "sit-ins" in early 1960. Young Negro college students led most of these demonstrations in Alabama, under the guidance of Dr. King. Theaters, beaches and other transportation facilities will soon be subject to the same "sit-in" kind of pressure in Alabama.

INTERRACIAL MARRIAGE

Alabama law forbids marriage between white and Negro.

ALASKA

"As one of the two newest states of the Union, it is important that the establishment of self-government in Alaska be done with maximum attention to the rights of its individual citizens."

ALASKA ADVISORY COMMITTEE,
U.S. COMMISSION ON CIVIL RIGHTS

Alaska, both the largest and the most northern of the fifty states, has made notable progress toward the elimination of discrimination in almost all significant areas. This, despite the fact that it has inherited a special problem—the presence in the state of over 37,000 natives whose ethnic, social, cultural and linguistic background differs profoundly from that of the white population. The vast expanse of Alaska and the sparseness of the population together with the corollary need for new settlers have perhaps contributed to creating a warm climate of public opinion toward all immigrants to the cold North.

VOTING

The eligibility to vote in Alaska is based upon a minimum age of 19 years and literacy in the English language. Despite the language qualification, there have been no complaints about deprivation of the voting privilege by natives, whites, or Negroes.

EDUCATION

Approximately 11% of the population of Alaska is composed of natives (Eskimo, Indian, Aleut, etc.) and 2½% of Negroes. In addition to the state-supported school system, the United States Bureau of Indian Affairs maintains a separate school system for native children. A student must be at least one-sixteenth native in order to be admitted to the latter. But as in many villages these are the only schools available, the law is liberally interpreted so that white or Negro children are not deprived of educational equality.

Little factual evidence as to the difference in quality of either the teaching staffs or standards of the two systems has been uncovered. Difficulties in transferring from native schools to state public schools appears to be due to other factors than discrimination. Problems of adjusting to a strange environment, loss of parental control, and language difficulties are some of these. In order to attend high school, for example, native children have to move to the major population centers or apply for admission to one of the two boarding schools for natives at Sitka or Mount Edgecomb. Unquestionably a dual school system will have to be supported by Alaska if the Eskimos are to retain their traditional mode of life which they show every inclination to do.

EMPLOYMENT

Alaska has had a Fair Employment Practices Act since 1952. The law recognizes the opportunity to obtain employment without discrimination as a civil right. Social clubs, fraternal, charitable, educational and religious associations and corporations, "not organized for private profit," are not subject to the statute. Employers with one or more employees are subject to the provisions of the FEPC which is administered by the State Department of Labor. There are penal provisions for violation of the law.

Formal complaints have been lodged by the Alaska Native Board on a number of occasions concerning discrimination against natives in the construction industry. Testimony, however, has seemed to indicate that this discrimination has resulted primarily because of a lack of technical training on the part of the natives that puts them at a disadvantage when competing with professional construction workers from other areas.

In Anchorage and Fairbanks, Negroes have made a number of complaints regarding the discrimination practiced by certain unions including Electrical Workers, Iron Workers, Plumbers, Operating Engineers and others. The unions were accused of excluding Negroes from both membership and participation in apprentice-training programs. Exclusion from union membership automatically deprives the excluded worker from employment opportunity in closed-shop situations. Both the unions and the major managements involved chose not to accept an invitation by the Civil Rights Commission to a hearing in Anchorage about a number of these discriminatory practice charges. Further investigation of the substance of the charges is under way.

HOUSING

The absence of relevant studies and statistics makes it difficult to evaluate the actual occurrence of discrimination in housing. The existence of "island communities" in major cities appears to be due to a combination of economic and cultural factors as well as to certain subtle discriminatory practices.

Numerous complaints have been brought before the Civil Rights Commission by minority citizens regarding the unavailability of rental units in government-financed apartments and/or private-home apartments. This type of discrimination undoubtedly exists. It should be noted, however, that two recent complaints about home financing finally revealed no discrimination as the applicants were found to be financially unqualified for the loans.

Urban renewal has been slow and inadequate in Alaska. Nevertheless, some programs have been carried out in sections of high Negro or native concentration. Certainly the absence of either state or local laws covering minority housing, or even recognizing the existence of segregation in Alaskan housing, has prevented any successful attack on the problem in the past.

PUBLIC ACCOMMODATIONS

Discrimination in public accommodations in Alaska is minimal.

INTERRACIAL MARRIAGE

Alaska has no law prohibiting racial intermarriage.

ARIZONA

"Ultimately, they may realize the practical wisdom of the answer given by the late William Wrigley, Jr., when he was asked whether his new Arizona Biltmore Hotel would conform to local traditions and bar Jewish guests. Replied Wrigley: 'Why should we? Jews chew gum, don't they?' "

HAROLD BRAVERMAN, *Bigotry and Hotels, Barriers*

Many resort hotels have developed "split personalities" because of the conflict between business necessity and discriminatory tradition.

Arizona inns, for example, had until recently a one-season operation, dedicated exclusively to the accommodation of individual
vacationing guests. The policy of many of these hotels of the South-
west was "Gentiles only." Mounting costs forced these establishments to solicit off-season convention business to survive. But hotels
that banned Jewish guests soon discovered that virtually all of the
trade and professional groups that held conventions included Jewish members and were not disposed to use facilities with a discriminatory policy. The inn-keepers extricated themselves from this
dilemma by admitting Jews as convention participants in the off-
season while continuing to exclude them during the vacation season.

The Camelback Inn at Phoenix is one famous Arizona hostelry
that has maintained a rigid "all-season" discriminatory policy despite formidable adverse publicity. Ever since the National Association of Attorney-Generals canceled its scheduled convention at
the Camelback in 1954 upon being informed of the hotel's "rigid
policy of 100% Gentile clientele," the Camelback has been the
object of a critical barrage. But neither the criticism nor the bad
publicity has changed Camelback policy. On the other hand, the
neighboring Arizona Biltmore (see above) in the same city has no
interest in the religious denomination of its guests.

VOTING

Discrimination in voting registration is prohibited in Arizona and
there have been no reported instances of such discrimination.

EDUCATION

Until 1951 segregation was permitted on the high school level and
mandatory at the elementary level in Arizona. Both practices were
repealed that year and actual desegregation began in Arizona (significantly) before the Supreme Court desegregation decision of 1954.
By 1958 all grades of the elementary and kindergarten levels had
become completely desegregated. Public high schools had accomplished it even earlier.

Indians and Spanish-Americans both far outnumber the Negroes
in Arizona. Most of the Indians live on reservations where they are

educated in federal schools. Since 1934 the federal government has been reimbursing school districts that accept Indian children from the reservations into the local public schools. Over 13,000 Indian children are in federal schools on the reservations, and 8,000 are in the state's public schools.

Many of the Mexican-Americans in Arizona are recent immigrants from Mexico whose adjustment is made more difficult by their ignorance of English. Both during and after the period of segregation, the language barrier had resulted in frequent segregation of Spanish-speaking pupils, especially in the lower grades. But this situation has greatly improved and today many Mexican-Americans are teaching in the public school system of Arizona.

EMPLOYMENT

A law barring discrimination in public employment was passed by the Arizona legislature in 1955. A bill is now pending before the legislature that would prohibit racial discrimination in the performance of contracts for public works. The bill appears to have been necessitated by instances of discrimination that have been reported.

HOUSING

The fact that Mexican-Americans and Indians live in segregated sections of the cities and towns in Arizona has been attributed to their low economic position. They are forced to be satisfied with substandard housing because they cannot afford anything better.

Negroes have no choice but to remain in or near segregated sections regardless of their economic position. Real estate agents and loan companies exert the leadership in Arizona housing practices.

PUBLIC ACCOMMODATIONS

Arizona has no laws either prohibiting or requiring discrimination or segregation by private enterprises. There is a good deal of evidence of discrimination against Negroes, Indians and Jews in the renting of hotel rooms and other services and accommodations. The policy of the Camelback Inn has already been referred to.

INTERRACIAL MARRIAGE

Arizona laws prohibited marriage between Caucasian and Negro, Hindu, Mongolian, Malayan or Indian until 1959. The Arizona State Superior Court in Tucson ruled in that year that the state statute violated both the state and federal constitutions.

ARKANSAS

". . . The Constitutional rights of children not to be discriminated against in school admission on grounds of race or color . . . can neither be nullified openly and directly by state legislators or state executive or judicial officers, nor nullified indirectly by them through evasive schemes for segregation, whether attempted 'ingeniously or ingenuously.' "

U.S. SUPREME COURT IN SUPPORT OF
ITS OWN SCHOOL SEGREGATION RULING

Little Rock, a point in time in the school desegregation battle, represents a frustration to both the Negro leadership and the white immoderates in the South. If the intention of the federal government to support the right of nine Negro students to attend their duly designated school was reaffirmed by the fly-in of 9,000 troops of the 1st Armored Division, it was, in the last analysis, satisfactory to neither party in the dispute. Arkansas whites learned of the tremendous power that the national government could apply to its will but they also learned the extent to which their state officials could combat and circumvent that will. The Negro petitioners for desegregation learned of the force of national public opinion that was behind them, but they also learned to what appalling extent their white neighbors bid them ill welcome, even in defiance of law and order and their own self-interest.

The Little Rock violence has dominated and changed every aspect of race relations in Arkansas since 1957.

VOTING

Arkansas is one of the five states that make the payment of a poll tax a prerequisite to voting. The state has no registration as such. Payment of the poll tax is the equivalent of registration.

In 1958 the total number of registered voters in Arkansas was 563,978. Of this total, 499,955 were white and 64,023 were nonwhite. Nonwhites, therefore, were 11.4% of all registered voters. These nonwhite registered voters represented 28.1% of the total population of voting-age nonwhites.

Arkansas has 75 counties. In 14 of them no Negroes were registered. In 29 of them from 1 to 25% of eligible Negroes were registered. Although Negroes represented the voting-age majority of the population in six Arkansas counties, in only 4 of these were more than 50% of the Negroes registered to vote.

EDUCATION

The convulsive crisis that gripped the Arkansas school system on September 2, 1957, shows few signs of abating. Desegregation is now in effect in nine school districts in the state. Little Rock's four high schools, closed for a year, reopened almost a month early last year with token desegregation. Ozark was dropped and Pulaski was added to the list of desegregated districts. Governor Orville Faubus suffered a defeat on a bond proposal but it is too early to determine if the sentiment for education, even if desegregated, or unalterable opposition to any desegregation will prevail in Arkansas.

A federal court pointed out that 3,665 pupils were affected by the closing of the Little Rock schools in 1958–59. Of these, 266 white and 376 Negro students did not subsequently attend any schools. The others obtained a variety of formal instruction in public and private schools both within and without the state.

EMPLOYMENT

Arkansas has no law applying to discrimination in private or public employment. Employment opportunities do not exist for Negroes in the state except in low-paying service and agricultural jobs. Many Negroes migrate out of Arkansas to northern industrial centers.

Arkansas' ambitious industrialization program which, before Little Rock, was making amazing progress in liberating the economy of the state from its dependence upon agriculture has now come to almost a complete standstill, according to the *Wall Street Journal* and *Fortune*.

HOUSING

The Negro population of Arkansas is concentrated in two general areas. One is the eastern cotton-growing belt along the Mississippi River. In these counties the population ranges from 48 to 67% Negro. The second area embraces the southern counties along the Louisiana and Texas borders, where the Negro population varies from about 27 to 45% of the whole. Segregation in both of these sections is complete. Housing is indisputably the field where Negro-white relations in Arkansas are least susceptible to imminent change.

PUBLIC ACCOMMODATIONS

The state continues to attempt the maintenance of mandatory segregation in transportation and recreational facilities. But as of September, 1961, "sit-in" campaigns had already desegregated variety stores, lunch-counters in Fort Smith and Little Rock. "Freedom Rides" have integrated bus terminals in Newport, Conway and Little Rock. Further modification of public accommodation practices in Arkansas would seem to have to follow legal desegregation in more public areas such as education and employment.

INTERRACIAL MARRIAGE

The state prohibits marriage between white and Negro.

CALIFORNIA

"It was partly due to what the kids hear about racial clashes on the outside and partly because recently a large group of Negroes were sent here and the Mexicans were outnumbered by both Negroes and whites for the first time."

SUPT. PAUL J. MC KUSICK OF THE CALIFORNIA YOUTH AUTHORITY,
MAY 25, 1961

The violent race riot between Mexican and Negro youths at California's biggest institution for juvenile offenders, that Supt. McKusick was commenting upon, is a vivid symbol of the involved nature of California's racial problem.

Various forms of discrimination based on race, religion or national origin are complicated in California because of the large number of minority groups in the state. These groups include over 500,000 Negroes, 800,000 Mexican-Americans, 85,000 Japanese-Americans, 60,000 Chinese-Americans, 450,000 Jews, over 2,000,-000 Catholics and a million foreign-born.

Not only does California present the usual racial tensions between whites and Negroes but the state is also host to a number of frictions such as described above between Negroes and Mexican-Americans. Residual feelings from the Sino-Japanese war likewise color the relations between the state's Japanese-American and Chinese-American minorities.

During the "swastika epidemic" that swept the United States in 1960, California suffered the highest incidence of these desecrations of Jewish temples and community buildings, according to the Anti-Defamation League of B'nai B'rith.

But civil rights progress has been apparent in certain areas in recent years. Most notable, perhaps, has been the gradual integration of the Japanese-Americans into the white community—after years of discrimination during and immediately following World War II.

VOTING

California law prohibits discrimination against voters because of race, religion or color. There is no basis for complaint in the administration of voting registration.

EDUCATION

Through many years of vigorous legislative action and public education, California has effectively sought to eliminate racial discrimination at the student level in the state schools and colleges. Discrimination in teacher employment does exist in many of California's school districts, however.

It is the opinion of the California State Advisory Committee of the U.S. Commission on Civil Rights that Negro candidates experience the greatest difficulty of all minorities in securing teaching positions in California. Teachers of Oriental descent have had increasingly greater access to such jobs in the last few years. A few California schools districts still do not hire Jews or Catholics as teachers but, by and large, this form of discrimination is ending.

A section of the California code declares it to be against the public policy to refuse or fail to recommend teachers for employment because of race, creed, color or national origin. The demonstrable failure of this legislation in some areas has led to the establishment of a Commission on Discrimination in Teacher Employment "to assist and advise local school districts."

EMPLOYMENT

The consensus of all studies and surveys of California employment is that 60% of the state's employers practice some kind of discriminatory policy based on race, religion or national origin. Among other criteria, the median wage of the nonwhite is little more than half that of the median white wage. Failure to promote minority employees to jobs for which they are qualified has been frequently noted. A case of this nature last year involving the Santa Fe Railroad resulted in an FEPC order reinstating a carman who, it was found, had been denied promotion on discriminatory grounds. California has had an FEPC Act since 1959 but, as in the case with educational discrimination, the law has often been ahead of community sentiment.

Many firms in Los Angeles still specify in their job orders for clerical workers that Jews, Negroes, Orientals, Mexican-Americans and Catholics need not apply. The California FEPC dealt with nearly 700 complaints of this type of discrimination in its first 17 months.

HOUSING

Despite the illegality under California law of restrictive covenants, many builders, lending institutions, and realty boards have entered into "gentlemen's agreements" to sell only to certain racial and religious groups. In some areas of southern California minority groups are deprived of equal opportunity to purchase homes in new subdivisions whose financing is guaranteed by the FHA. To buy a home at all they are forced to pay almost double the amount of mortgage financing. Racial discrimination in renting is practiced openly in California. Efforts are now being made to extend the legal provisions against housing discrimination that have so far proved inadequate.

PUBLIC ACCOMMODATIONS

Discrimination, including segregation, in transportation and recreational facilities is prohibited by law in California. The record of the administration of justice of this policy, as in California's other areas of discrimination, is less impressive than the intent of the law.

INTERRACIAL MARRIAGE

A California statute banning interracial marriage was declared unconstitutional in 1948.

COLORADO

"It can be fairly estimated that the State of Colorado has 200,000 people with Spanish names or 11.6% of the population."

The Denver Post

As 10% seems to be the classical proportion at which a minority group becomes a major recipient of discriminatory practices, it is perhaps not surprising that Americans with Spanish names and of Mexican descent bear the main burden of such practices in Colorado. Despite the fact that the state also contains 27,000 Jews, 24,000 Negroes, 2,500 Japanese-Americans and 5,000 Indians, it is the Mexican-Americans, particularly the 150,000 who live away from metropolitan Denver, that represent the greatest statewide problem in civil rights.

Another grave problem is that of the migratory worker. The Colorado State Employment Service has estimated that there are about 14,000 of these who come into the state to work at Colorado's seasonal harvesting. Approximately 2,000 are Mexican nationals but over 7,000 are American citizens, predominantly of Mexican descent. They represent a serious civil rights problem, of course, because they live without protection from either federal, state or local laws. Migrant workers and their families can be, and are, discriminated against in education (few of their children stay in one place long enough to attend school), employment (minimum-wage laws do not cover migratory employment and these workers receive shockingly low wages), and housing (they must live in "company" housing). Lately, Colorado state agencies, counties, and many individuals have come to recognize a moral responsibility to help the migratory worker and his family.

VOTING

Colorado laws prohibit discrimination in voting and they have been almost universally enforced. There is no evidence of discrimination in this area.

EDUCATION

Discrimination and segregation are prohibited in the state's public schools. There is virtually no instance of discrimination in higher education as all high schools, colleges, universities and technical institutes admit all qualified applicants regardless of race, color or creed.

EMPLOYMENT

A Fair Employment Practices Act was adopted in 1957 which is administered by the Colorado Anti-Discrimination Commission. Negotiation and mediation are emphasized although courts may be requested to issue "cease and desist" orders. Of the first 140 cases dealt with by the commission only three necessitated such court orders. The Colorado commission is handicapped, as are many, by a small budget and small staff.

Only employers of six or more employees are subject to the provisions of the FEPC act. A bill to amend the existing law to include all employers was defeated by a vote of 20–15 in the state senate in February, 1961.

The prevailing wage for seasonal migratory agricultural workers has been 65 cents an hour in several parts of Colorado such as the rich Arkansas Valley. It has been even lower in others. A number of laudable but uncoordinated efforts have been initiated to alleviate the condition of the migratory workers. Fort Lupton and Palisade are generally recognized as good labor camps. The Colorado Migrant Ministry of the Colorado Council of Churches and the National Council of Catholic Women have been particularly devoted to the care of the dependents of the labor force. A well-planned program of teaching the children of the migrants has been put into effect by the Colorado State Department of Education. It is acknowledged by everyone concerned that a far greater mobilization of the state's authority is needed to cope with the migratory problem.

HOUSING

The Colorado Fair Housing Act was signed by Governor McNichols on April 10, 1959. This act prohibits discrimination in all types of housing, private as well as public and publicly-aided. Colorado has thus gone further than any other state in the Union in prohibiting discrimination in housing. In fact, only two cities in the country— New York and Pittsburgh—have adopted similarly comprehensive antidiscriminatory housing ordinances. The act is administered by the Colorado Anti-Discrimination Commission.

However, a ghetto situation would still probably fairly describe the living conditions of 95% of Denver's Negroes. There is also considerable evidence of discrimination in the renting, sale and purchase of homes and apartments to the Mexican and Jewish minority groups. The Colorado Advisory Committee to the U.S. Commission on Civil Rights believes that if the Anti-Discrimination Commission administers the new act "with the same wisdom it has shown in handling FEPC, considerable progress should be made in this field."

It should be noted that an Urban League film strip dramatizing Negro pride and conscientiousness in home ownership has had a salutary effect in shaping local attitudes.

PUBLIC ACCOMMODATIONS

Colorado adopted a public accommodations law barring discrimination in the use of all public facilities and conveniences as early as 1895. The Anti-Discrimination Commission has found no evidence of discrimination by theaters or in public transportation. Public swimming pools and golf courses in Denver are open to members of all ethnic groups and this seems to be the case in most areas of Colorado. Interestingly, better class hotels and restaurants have been found relatively free of discrimination while poorer class establishments have not.

A recent survey of motels in the Denver area revealed that 46% of those interviewed admitted to some discriminatory practices. This anomaly between the liberal spirit of the law and the two standards in practice is partially explained by the fact that Colorado resorts entertain a substantial number of southern visitors who, it is felt, exercise some influence upon their hosts.

INTERRACIAL MARRIAGE

Colorado laws prohibit marriage between whites and Negroes.

CONNECTICUT

"Evidence indicates that integration proceeds fairly rapidly in the area of childhood play activities. Younger children are less conscious of the social implications of color difference, and their parents, on the whole, view interracial play activities with favor. Parents seemed to be aware of their own prejudicial upbringing when many of them told us that they felt interracial play activities would be good for their children's future understanding of interracial problems. This racial interaction continues in the schools, as evidenced by the high degree of integration achieved in Connecticut both in curricular and extra-curricular activities. Interaction on these age levels undoubtedly holds the greatest promise for the future."

HENRY G. STETLER, SUPERVISOR, RESEARCH DIVISION,
CONNECTICUT COMMISSION ON CIVIL RIGHTS,
Private Interracial Neighborhoods in Connecticut

Connecticut's approach to many of the civil rights problems it shares with other northern states is characterized by being both unique and effective. The state has established a strong Civil Rights

Commission and authorized it not only with enforcement powers but also with a significant mandate to conduct research into the real causes and solutions of interracial tensions. The Connecticut Civil Rights Commission has been responsible for a whole series of imaginative but practical studies in the area of civil rights such as *Private Interracial Neighborhoods in Connecticut, Attitudes Toward Racial Integration in Connecticut,* and others that have played a salutary part in preparing both the state's officials and citizens for integration.

VOTING

There has been no reported discrimination in Connecticut voting.

EDUCATION

Public education has been available in Connecticut to members of all races on an integrated basis since 1868. But the problems of Negro students who attend integrated schools yet go home to segregated neighborhoods has resulted in a dilution of the benefits that the young Negroes could have been receiving from integrated education, according to the Connecticut Commission on Civil Rights which has analyzed this development, particularly as it has manifested itself in "drop-outs."

"Drop-outs"—high school students who leave school before graduation and thereby severely limit their earning capacity in later years—appear more frequently among Negro students than whites because of the debilitating effects of discriminatory factors in other aspects of their life, according to the commission. Ways and means of educating "drop-outs" to stay in or return to school are being studied.

EMPLOYMENT

The Connecticut Commission on Civil Rights protects minority group workers in the state from employment discrimination. There remain, of course, many instances of discrimination in hiring and promotion, but as the commission's work includes an educational program for employers and citizens, Connecticut Negroes at least have the knowledge that this problem is being confronted.

HOUSING

It was estimated, as of 1956, that Connecticut's Negro population was housed in approximately 16,000 dwelling units, about one-fourth in integrated public housing projects. Except for an insignificant few, the Negroes not in the new projects live in homes and neighborhoods decidedly inferior to those occupied by whites. The Connecticut Commission on Civil Rights, in one of its research studies, reports (in *Private Interracial Neighborhoods in Connecticut*):

"The process of breaking the racial barrier in private residential neighborhoods creates a series of problems, accompanied by formidable obstacles, for Negro families.

"The initial problem involves the act of securing a place to live in a previously all-white neighborhood. If successful, and if not followed by a flight of white and an influx of other Negro families, the section becomes nonsegregated in character. At this stage, nonsegregation means simply that Negro families live contiguous to their white neighbors. It does not necessarily mean that the Negro families have become *integrated* in the neighborhood. This distinction is crucial because of the frequent assumption that the mere presence of Negroes in an interracial situation implies integration in the group."

PUBLIC ACCOMMODATIONS

Connecticut's Public Accommodation Law makes it illegal to refuse any person full and equal service in a public place because of race, creed or color. But even with this liberal and comprehensive legislation, certain unattained goals remain for the state's minority citizens.

INTERRACIAL MARRIAGE

The State has no law banning interracial marriage.

DELAWARE

"In Wilmington, where the desegregation program was extended to the junior high school level and the transfer policy liberalized at the high school level, a Negro boy was elected president of the junior class of the newly desegregated Pierre S. du Pont High School."

Southern School News, NOV. 1955

The border state of Delaware is divided by its own "Mason-Dixon" line, the Chesapeake and Delaware Canal, into northern and southern sections that remarkably illustrate national, northern and southern attitudes toward civil rights. The northern half has so far taken a number of notable strides toward desegregation while the southern half of the state has been almost as recalcitrant as the Deep South.

Delaware affords several interesting examples of the problems involved in the desegregation of Negro institutions. Delaware State College, established in 1871 for colored students, had been so neglected by succeeding legislatures that a Governor's Committee recommended its closing in 1950. However, after an increased appropriation from the state and a thorough reorganization, the college was able to continue and even secure reaccreditation by 1957. Nevertheless, only four to ten white students have enrolled each year since 1954 and these have been, for the most part, servicemen from the nearby Dover Air Force Base. The first white student was graduated in 1957 and the 1960 enrollment included six white students among a total of 356.

VOTING

There are no racial, religious or national origin restrictions on the right to vote in Delaware. Even the southern half of the state has a record of unrestricted voting registration.

EDUCATION

Twenty-six of 51 biracial school districts in Delaware have been desegregated under the grade-a-year state-wide plan approved by a federal court. All of the cities north of Delaware's "Mason-Dixon" line quickly announced and steadily implemented plans of desegregation after the Supreme Court decision. The only two cities south of the line that attempted even plans of limited desegregation were the state capital Dover and Milford.

The Milford experience is regarded as an excellent illustration on how not to prepare a community for desegregation of the public schools. No advance notice was given the Milford citizens and the school personnel were not given any particular policy or directive. Also no desegregation of public accommodations had preceded the school desegregation; the only formula that had been found effective in the southern Delaware scene. Organized public protest forced the school board to close the Milford school only one week after the desegregated term had begun. Eventually a new school board was elected and it expelled the Negro students. This ended Milford's desegregation. In striking contrast was the story of school desegregation in Newark, Delaware, only a few miles north of Milford where public protest was swiftly and firmly controlled by official determination. Newark is now desegregated. This swift accomplishment was immensely facilitated by the efforts of private groups, particularly the local United Auto Workers organization.

EMPLOYMENT

In July 1960 Delaware became the 17th state to adopt a fully-enforceable FEPC law. In his inaugural address Governor Carvel asked that the FEPC act be given the tools of money and staff so it might "implement the authority given it." There is considerable evidence of discrimination in Delaware employment, most frequently in the southern part of the state.

HOUSING

The housing situation for Negroes in Delaware has been progressively deteriorating in the decade between 1950 and 1960. Despite the increase in Negro population during this period the relative number of dwelling units occupied by Negroes declined—while the relative number of units occupied by whites increased. Negroes are inevitably being driven into neighborhoods that are substandard and often without sanitary services, suitable water supply or other services. Negroes are unable to acquire decent housing in well-established neighborhoods because of strict segregation. The State of Delaware has no discernible policy in this area.

PUBLIC ACCOMMODATIONS

Northern Delaware is proceeding at a slow but regular pace in the desegregation of public transportation, parks, libraries and swimming pools. South of the Chesapeake and Delaware Canal few gestures have been made to alter the traditional segregation in public accommodations.

Delaware Negroes are either excluded or admitted only conditionally to most of the professional and business associations. The policies of the State Board examinations are held largely responsible for this: many Negro applicants who fail to become certified in Delaware professional societies are often subsequently recognized by boards in other states.

INTERRACIAL MARRIAGE

Delaware prohibits marriage between white and Negro.

DISTRICT OF COLUMBIA

"Five years have passed since the District of Columbia schools began the process of desegregation. Today the main object of study, debate and effort is how to make the schools better."

CARL F. HANSEN, SUPT. OF SCHOOLS, WASHINGTON, D.C.

The five-year desegregation of schools in the nation's capital is generally regarded as a brilliant model of how to accomplish such a transformation in a community, both with deliberate speed and full consideration for all segments of the community involved. The Washington experience cannot be regarded as typical because, of course, it took place in the capital. But Washington is a southern city with southern mores; it has a large population majority of Negroes, and it has, today, a desegregated school system.

National publicity focused on two other aspects of discrimination during 1961. Attorney General Robert Kennedy's resignation called attention to the long established discrimination of the city's most prominent club, The Metropolitan, against Negro members or guests. And world attention was drawn to the inability of African envoys to secure suitable housing in the capital. Both of these situations, it is believed, are in the process of change.

VOTING

Until the last session of Congress, no resident of the District of Columbia could vote in either local or national elections. This restriction, originally drawn to prevent the development of a large "spoils-system" electorate in the national capital, has now been amended to permit D.C. residents to vote for President and Vice President in national elections. In any case, it appears that because of recent developments, District of Columbia residents will no longer share with some American minority groups in certain southern areas the distinction of not enjoying universal suffrage.

EDUCATION

At the time it began, directly after the Supreme Court desegregation decision, the desegregation of the Washington schools was by no means assured of success. There was a very strong hostility among white parents and a very real problem of an overwhelming Negro student majority. The success of the Washington plan is universally attributed to Superintendent Hansen and his staff and teachers. The Washington desegregation involved radical transfers of pupils, teachers and plant facilities. Vexing problems of all kinds had to be met because desegregation of the school system was not, of course, accompanied by desegregation of Washington's neighborhoods. Today, however, it is quite accurate to suggest, as Superin-

tendent Hansen has, that national educators' main interest in the
Washington school system is "how to make the schools better."
Desegregation is history.

EMPLOYMENT

Washington, as is well-known, is a company town; the company
being the United States Government. The federal government not
only dominates the employment landscape but under the Kennedy
Administration has begun a firm assault on prevailing southern discriminatory customs. There is still some evidence of discrimination
in the closely observed federal employment, however. Civil service
regulations guard all levels and conditions of government work.
With very little even light industry, Washington's private employment opportunities are primarily in the service and domestic categories. The expanding Negro population and the strong government
example are gradually widening the range of job opportunities for
the Negro. The fact that many national labor, business and political
associations are increasingly making their headquarters in the national capital also tends to increase employment possibilities for the
Negro. These organizations almost invariably hire without the
(southern) local bias.

HOUSING

The State Department announced on July 10, 1961 that the problem of housing African diplomats was largely solved. Protocol officers received a pledge that eight apartment buildings would there-
after be open to African envoys and their families. No treaty,
however, was announced between Washington realtors and American Negroes. The head of the Washington branch of the NAACP
said that he doubted that the problem would be totally solved until
there was legislation outlawing discrimination in all Washington
housing.

The blighted and impoverished residential downtown of Washington, within sight of the Capitol and the White House, has long
been the slum home of many Washington Negroes. Annual pilgrim-
ages by indignant legislators, accompanied by cameramen, have

not resulted in any significant urban renewal. There is a growing feeling that the unique charter under which the District of Columbia is governed by the federal government is itself responsible for much of the red tape that ensnarls plans for improvement and desegregation.

PUBLIC ACCOMMODATIONS

Certain discrimination in the national capital's private facilities has long been a notorious subject for world comment. There have been countless episodes, well-reported, of Negroes and Africans being denied meals and other services in the last few years. Under pressure from the Urban League, CORE, and the NAACP many discriminatory policies have been liberalized. Municipal transportation and other facilities are desegregated and inadequate for all races.

INTERRACIAL MARRIAGE

There is no law respecting intermarriage in the District of Columbia.

FLORIDA

"Prior to the bus protest, race relations in Tallahassee displayed a high degree of accommodation. No incidents of any consequence had occurred to disturb this apparent satisfactory adjustment for more than ten years. Because of this outward calm, the whites high in the power structure of Tallahassee were led to believe that the Negro in Tallahassee was satisfied."

Tallahassee Bus Protest
BY CHARLES U. SMITH AND LEWIS M. KILLIAN

June, 1956, definitely marks the date of a new era of race relations in Florida. The initiation of the Tallahassee bus boycott at that time changed the pattern of Negro "accommodation" to discrimination and segregation in the state. Becoming increasingly aware of their economic and political power, Florida Negroes have pressed for an extension of their civil rights on several fronts.

The desegregation of the Tallahassee buses was followed by successful sit-in campaigns that opened a large number of lunch counters and other public facilities throughout Florida. The NAACP, CORE and other national organizations have been active in the agitation for these goals. The young Negro college and high school students of the state rallied promptly behind this leadership. This development, as potent as it has been unexpected, has served strong notice upon both the state and the older Negro leadership that the pursuit of civil rights will continue to be a lively issue in Florida.

VOTING

According to 1958 state statistics approximately 40% of Florida Negroes over 21 were registered to vote. In 19 counties the figure was more than 50%. Dade and Duval Counties, where Miami and Jacksonville are located, together accounted for almost 50,000 of Florida's nearly 150,000 registered Negro voters. This is probably the highest proportion of registered Negro voters in the South, testifying to Florida's generally nondiscriminatory policy in this area. A certain few counties, however, have made it exceedingly difficult for Negroes to vote. Gadsden County, in Northern Florida on the Georgia border, is one out of five in the state's 67, in which less than 5% of the voting-age Negroes were registered. 348 Negroes were registered in Gadsden in 1960: 10,930 lived there. Sworn complaints to the U.S. Commission on Civil Rights cited intimidation and economic reprisal against Negroes who had attempted to register and urge others to register. Three other rural counties—Lafayette, Liberty and Union—had no Negroes registered in 1958.

One elderly Negro from the county who was interviewed by the commission said that he had registered about three years before but had decided not to vote. When asked why, he said, "I am too old to be beaten up."

EDUCATION

By September, 1960, seven Negro students had been enrolled at Florida graduate schools. The first white junior college in the state was also desegregated to the extent of admitting three Negroes during the same month.

An academic event of far greater importance than any of these previous admissions was the enrollment of about 50 Negro undergraduates in the University of Miami this summer. Twenty-six additional candidates will be accepted at the Coral Gables campus in the fall. This represents the lowering of the color bar at the largest independent college in the Southeast.

Florida law has required total segregation in all grades of the public school system. Pending court cases have a variety of the segregation statutes under challenge. Dade County (Miami) will integrate six more schools this fall, bringing the total to ten and increasing from 28 to about 250 the total number of Negroes in biracial public schools in Florida.

EMPLOYMENT

Equal employment opportunities remain one of the most unattainable goals of Florida Negroes. The Urban League of Jacksonville has waged a particularly tenacious struggle for better jobs. Their efforts were rewarded in the last year by several firsts that illustrate the League's steadfastness—and the magnitude of the task: the first Negro chain store manager, the first radio announcer, the first hat designer, the first police promotion of a Negro from patrolman to sergeant, the first hiring of Negro airline clerks.

HOUSING

Negro housing in Florida is completely segregated. Both state law and state tradition reinforce the total segregation.

One of Florida's better-known reputations is as a winter resort paradise. Certain parts of the southeastern, Miami, Atlantic beach paradise are for "Gentiles only." Delray Beach, 50 miles north of Miami, has excluded Jewish vacationers 100%. Fort Lauderdale has an average of 50 "restricted" outside signs advertising discrimination. Miami Beach also maintains a number of resort hotels that do not cater to Jewish travelers.

PUBLIC ACCOMMODATIONS

The only public accommodations that Florida Negroes can avail themselves of are those such as lunch counters and transportation facilities that they have desegregated by political and boycott action in the last few years. State law has been the instrument of mandatory segregation. In August of 1961, the state legislature passed a law banning "wade-ins."

INTERRACIAL MARRIAGE

Marriage between white and Negro is prohibited in Florida.

GEORGIA

"When people say a story should be suppressed for the good of the community, what they usually mean is peace at any price. We just don't believe in that."

CARL HOLMAN, EDITOR OF THE *Atlanta Inquirer*, A NEGRO NEWSPAPER

Atlanta, Georgia, the recognized capital of the Deep South, demonstrated on August 30, 1961, that careful preparation can prevent the violence that has heretofore characterized public school desegregation in this region. On that date 12 Negroes entered four previously white high schools in Atlanta. Their admission marked Georgia's first token step toward compliance with the Supreme Court's desegregation ruling of 1954.

School desegregation in Georgia left only South Carolina, Alabama and Mississippi in a posture of complete defiance. Opposition to even token compliance remains strong in the rural countryside but an unprecedented campaign of education and publicity in the city of Atlanta strengthened the support for peaceful desegregation.

Atlanta also, in a sense, has become the intellectual capital of the South. The presence in the city of men like Ralph McGill, publisher of the *Atlanta Constitution,* the universally respected Mayor William B. Hartsfield, and the acknowledged leader of the southern Negroes, the Reverend Martin Luther King, has contributed enormously to Atlanta's climate of public opinion. A number of voluntary organizations including HOPE (*Help Our Public Education*) and OASIS (*Organizations Assisting Schools In September*) have energetically pressed the open school campaign.

HOPE and OASIS are countered by a white citizens' group called GUTS (*Georgians Unwilling to Surrender*).

VOTING

The range of voting conditions and the degree of Negro participation in Georgia elections vary widely. The heaviest Negro voting is in urban-industrial areas. The Negro population exceeds 50% in 42 counties and is between 33% and 49% in 39 additional counties. On the other hand, in only 27 of the state's 159 counties were more than 50% of the voting-age Negroes registered in 1958. In Baker County, with some 1,800 Negroes of voting age, none was registered; in Lincoln County, only three out of more than 1,500; in Miller, six out of more than 1,300; in Terrell, 48 out of 5,000. In 22 counties with sizable Negro populations, fewer than 5% were registered.

In 1947 there were 125,000 Negroes registered in Georgia; in 1958, after the most strenuous efforts by Negro leaders, only 161,-082 had been registered.

The Georgia State Advisory Committee to the U.S. Commission

on Civil Rights commented on one form of the discrimination faced by would-be Negro voters:

"The 1958 session of the Georgia General Assembly passed a bill frankly designed to discourage Negro registrants. It poses 30 questions to the 'illiterate voter,' 20 of which must be answered correctly. Considerable discretion remains with the registrar in deciding who shall have to answer questions and whether the answers are correct . . ."

The committee also gave an example of a registrar's discretion. In Terrell County the chairman of the county board of registrars gave as grounds for denying registration to four Negro schoolteachers that in their reading test they "pronounced 'equity' as 'eequity,' and all had trouble with the word 'original.'" The chairman of the registrars said that he interpreted Georgia law to mean that applicants must "read so I can understand."

EDUCATION

Beginning in 1952 Georgia General Assemblies have passed a long list of laws designed to thwart integration of the school system to any degree. Many of these laws appear to contradict each other; application of others would appear to depend wholly on the interpretation of elected officials and the state attorney general. Twelve Negroes entered the 11th and 12th grades of Atlanta High School on August 30, 1961. The Atlanta community has given overwhelming support to this token desegregation.

Four private institutions of higher learning in the state, three of them Negro colleges, have adopted nondiscriminatory admission policies. The enrollment of two Negroes at the state's University of Georgia last January provoked riots that were controlled only with the greatest difficulty. However, a federal court insisted on the Negroes' admission and they have now been joined by a Negro woman graduate student who was accepted at the Athens campus this spring. Georgia Tech, the other famous institution in the state's university system, has accepted three Negro Atlanta high school students from among thirteen Negro applicants for admission in the fall of 1961. The Tech action is regarded as significant in that it is one of the few voluntary admissions in the Deep South. No court order was involved.

EMPLOYMENT

Marietta, Georgia, is the scene of the most determined and sustained drive for elimination of employment discrimination in the history of the South. Stirred by a story in Carl Holman's *Atlanta Inquirer* which pointed out a number of discriminatory practices at the Lockheed Aircraft Corporation's huge Marietta plant, national and, more importantly, White House attention focused upon Marietta. It was firmly established that Lockheed's provision of separate time clocks, dining and rest-room facilities for Negroes plus the company's undeniable record of racial restriction of jobs in the engineering, professional and supervisory categories were demonstrably illegal for a corporation working under a nondiscriminatory government contract.

When it became obvious that President Kennedy intended to use the Lockheed plant as a model in the government's drive to eliminate employment discrimination in all companies working on defense contracts, definite progress began. Lockheed has aircraft and missile contracts with the government amounting to an aggregate value of over one billion dollars. A pact was signed between Lockheed and the President's Committee on Equal Employment Opportunity, headed by Vice-President Johnson. Intensive efforts to wipe out discrimination have begun. A number of Negro employees have been upgraded in jobs and others enrolled in apprentice training programs. All traces of dual facilities in the plant have been eliminated. The reaction of the white community, which was feared as a strong braking factor, has been tolerant and resigned. Apparently the realization that violent reaction would have forced Lockheed— which could hardly afford to jeopardize all of its government contracts for the Marietta operation—out of Georgia, was the determining factor.

Exclusive of the Lockheed experience, Negroes in Georgia are still the recipients of the most acute type of employment discrimination.

HOUSING

As a whole Georgia is low in Negro home ownership, heavy in relatively high-priced, substandard rental quarters. Savannah and other older cities have considerable "unplanned integration" in housing. The city's former slave quarters and carriage houses behind the big homes are now occupied by Negro families. Because of Mayor Hartsfield's administration, Atlanta is a unique situation. Housing is segregated but Negro home ownership is encouraged by municipal authorities. Negroes cannot obtain any loans elsewhere as easily as they can in Atlanta.

PUBLIC ACCOMMODATIONS

The well-reported sit-in movement that blazed into the news in February of 1960 was led in Georgia by the NAACP and many of the Negro churches in the state. It served to dramatize the state of public accommodations in Georgia. Until the sit-ins, Georgia had mandatory segregation in all transportation and most recreational facilities. The private sector of accommodation was even more rigidly segregated. A noteworthy number of eating places, public terminal facilities, department stores and places of public amusement have been opened as a result of the sit-in campaign. An arrangement was arrived at between the leadership of the Negro community and the Atlanta Chamber of Commerce to delay the Negro campaign for desegregation of public accommodations in Atlanta until the opening of the desegregated 11th and 12th grades in the Atlanta public schools this fall. At that time the merchants involved will voluntarily desegregate their facilities.

INTERRACIAL MARRIAGE

Marriage is prohibited between white and nonwhite in Georgia.

HAWAII

"Any politician of the slightest sagacity soon learns, if he does not already know, that the surest route to political suicide . . . (in Hawaii) . . . is an appeal on a racial basis."

DR. ANDREW W. LIND, *Racial Bloc Voting in Hawaii,*
UNIVERSITY OF HAWAII

It is a reflection of the genuine racial integration that has existed for many years in the youngest of the United States that such a statement as Professor Lind's can be made. The spirit of the quotation is not peculiar only to the voting habits of Hawaiians. Intermarriage between members of different ethnic groups has been, and is, common in Hawaii and has produced a great number of the leaders, in every field, of the new state.

Social acceptance, without regard to race, color or creed, has not always been the general rule in regard to several of the Oriental racial strains in Hawaii. But it is rapidly becoming the general rule. And it should be commented that the Hawaiian achievement has been attained, not by legislative action, judicial decree or executive fiat, but by the experience of the many races living and working together for many years.

VOTING

The franchise has been freely open to Hawaiians, without discrimination, since the earliest days of the Territory. Racial "bloc" voting, which often occurred in the Territory, as the only practical means of the respective minorities to express their political power, is now nonexistent in the state since integration has been achieved.

EDUCATION

Hawaii's educational system is completely integrated on all levels and there is no evidence of discrimination in any area. Elementary and secondary instruction are administered by the Department of Public Instruction whose seven commissioners are appointed by the governor with the consent of the senate. An American of Japanese descent is the present chairman, four of the members are white, one Chinese, and one of Swedish-Hawaiian descent. Sixty-five per cent of the nearly 5,000 teachers in the school system are nonwhite.

Japanese-Americans constitute the largest minority attending the University of Hawaii. The faculty of the university includes both men and women of Caucasian, Japanese, Chinese, Korean, Philippine and Hawaiian descent. There are no discriminatory restrictions of any kind in any of the university facilities and no student clubs are permitted to have racial codes.

EMPLOYMENT

Racial discrimination in employment has largely been eliminated in Hawaii. As the educational base of the entire population is broadened, the former condition of various minorities being *de facto* relegated to certain traditional employment categories (such as the Japanese-American in fruit-growing) has radically changed. There are pockets of segregated employment patterns but they are steadily decreasing.

No racial discrimination whatsoever exists in government employment in Hawaii.

HOUSING

Complete racial integration in public housing throughout Hawaii has been an established fact since the formation of the Hawaiian Housing Authority in 1935. There are no qualifications for tenancy based upon race, creed, color or point of national origin.

There is currently little evidence of bias in private housing. This has not always been the case. During the Territorial period it is probable that housing was the area of greatest discrimination and segregation in Hawaii. Particular neighborhoods in the cities and townships in the island countryside were tacitly reserved for specific minorities. The breakdown of this pattern has been hastened by statehood and the growing opportunities for educational and financial parity. ·

PUBLIC ACCOMMODATIONS

A few of the old, oligarchic island social clubs continue to limit their membership to white "mainlanders." Even this variety of private discrimination is diminishing, however.

All Hawaiian restaurants, theaters, hotels, public parks, public beaches and swimming pools, public golf courses and tennis courts are integrated. One restaurant in Honolulu was reported practicing social discrimination a number of years ago.

The interisland airlines, railroad and bus facilities have never been the subject of any charges of discrimination.

INTERRACIAL MARRIAGE

Hawaiians of all races intermarry.

IDAHO

"It will be recalled that during World War II enemy aliens thought to be dangerous were placed in internment camps and that all Japanese-American citizens on the west coast were shut up in 'War Relocation Centers.' These World War II policies were more or less ad hoc, and we do not regard them now with much pride and satisfaction."

ROBERT E. CUSHMAN, *Civil Liberties in the United States*

One of the more unlikely results of America's first modern experiment with concentration camp segregation during the war was the first sizable settlement of Japanese-Americans in the state of Idaho. Never comfortable with the detention policy, the government eventually began paroling loyal Japanese-Americans to "non-security" areas in the interior.

It can hardly be claimed that the Japanese-Americans who have stayed in Idaho during the twenty years since their bitter experience have been assimilated into the life of that state. Discrimination and segregation remain the Idaho reality. But at least one citizen of such descent has become a member of the Idaho State Advisory Committee to the U.S. Commission on Civil Rights and there have been minor penetrations of public accommodation traditions. It must be remarked that Idaho has been unique for decades in having almost no minority groups. Negroes have been and are an insignificant fraction of the population. Even the Indian tribes in Idaho have been a relatively less pressing problem than in other western states. The lack of industry and urban opportunity in Idaho until recently has been responsible for this isolation. Desegregated Army and Air Force installations in the state have been accepted without strife but have had an unknown impact on public opinion.

VOTING

The state constitution of Idaho provides that "Chinese or persons of Mongolian descent, not born in the United States, shall not vote." This is a holdover from the era of Oriental exclusion in the early West and is not believed capable of passing a court test.

EDUCATION

Religious tests are prohibited in public schools in Idaho. Segregation is prohibited. A survey of the colleges and universities of the state has indicated that there are no race problems of consequence among either students or teachers. The nonwhite enrollment in Idaho schools is very small. All-Indian enrollment at the elementary school in Power County is accounted for by the fact that there are no whites living in the area.

EMPLOYMENT

Idaho has no law barring discrimination in private employment. A lack of data on the actual employment practices of the state appears to result as much from the small number of minority residents as from the admittedly discriminatory tradition.

HOUSING

The Chairman of the Idaho State Advisory Committee to the U.S. Commission on Civil Rights reported that banks, building and loan agencies had assured him that there is no racial discrimination in Idaho housing. Indians living in tepees, the Chairman declared, are there by choice rather than necessity, and Negroes live in cheap rent sections only because they cannot afford better.

PUBLIC ACCOMMODATIONS

No law prohibiting or requiring discrimination or segregation by private enterprises exists in Idaho. It is generally recognized that Indians and Mexican-American migratory workers are denied admission to certain restaurants and taverns.

INTERRACIAL MARRIAGE

Marriage was prohibited between white and Mongolian or Negro in Idaho until the statute's repeal in March of 1960.

ILLINOIS

"When Commander Shepard climbed out of his space capsule after his historic flight, he learned that the school board of Deerfield, Illinois, had named its new junior high school the Alan B. Shepard School. Deerfield was last in the news when the all-white Chicago suburb tried to prevent a developer from building a project in the suburb because ten of the houses were to be sold to Negroes."

HARRY FLEISCHMAN, *Fact and Fiction,* AMERICAN JEWISH COMMITTEE

Chicago's chronic racial tension was aggravated during the last year by a number of serious outbreaks. A humanitarian expedition by the Red Cross, for instance, to guide 110 Negro victims of a slum fire to overnight shelter in a church in a nearby white neighborhood precipitated a riot by a mob who feared the Negroes were "moving in." Housing continues to be the most inflamed area of civil rights strife in Chicago and all of Illinois.

The aroused reaction of Deerfield to the possibility of ten Negro families entering the suburb was also inflamed.

Other elements of Illinois public opinion have strongly supported the desegregation of the Negro community as the best hope for the eventual end of the state's racial unrest. Certainly the Illinois political leaders of both parties have been ahead of their constituencies in seeking ways and means to achieve civil rights progress. The unceasing stream of southern Negroes into the overcrowded, ghetto-like conditions of the Illinois urban centers dictates that a solution to the situation of the Negro in Illinois is urgent.

Southern Illinois, predominantly rural, has maintained many Southern customs in regard to treatment of Negroes.

VOTING

There is no discrimination in the accessibility of the right to register and vote in Illinois. Residence requirements often discourage Negro registration, especially in the state's southern counties, but this is difficult to document.

EDUCATION

Statutes prohibiting segregation in the public schools of Illinois have existed since 1874. A survey conducted by the Illinois Commission on Human Relations in 1950 established that in only one city, Chicago, were Negro teachers employed in integrated or all-white schools. The same survey taken ten years later revealed that 31 Illinois cities then employed Negro teachers in integrated school systems. Twenty-three of these cities employ more than one.

Sixteen institutions of higher learning reported in a survey that they did not practice policies of racial exclusion. Only one reported all white students. All the senior colleges of the sampling and five junior colleges indicated their enrollments included three races.

Off-campus housing and fraternity and sorority discrimination are features of Illinois university life that have been impervious to administrative and legislative suggestion.

EMPLOYMENT

A Chicago social agency has unequivocally stated that at least 1,500 companies in the metropolitan area practice racial or religious discrimination in hiring. Another six month study of employment agency procedures illustrated that although 46% of all Protestant applicants and 39% of all Catholics were placed, only 12% of all Jews and 1.3% of all Negro applicants were similarly fortunate. And this was one of the very few employment agencies in Chicago that attempt to place white-collar Negro job-seekers.

Four reports on apprenticeship programs have indicated that no Negroes were in apprenticeship in Chicago, Joliet and Champaign at the time of the study. Reasons advanced included union opposition. Successive studies, reports and evaluations by local, state and private agencies have corroborated the extent of racial discrimination in Illinois employment. The state has no FEPC.

HOUSING

Seventy-five per cent of Chicago's Negroes live in 7 of the city's 75 neighborhoods, the most famous of which add up to the South Side. Volatile racial incidents periodically erupt in the sections where Negroes move into previously white communities. Since World War II, three large-scale riots have occurred in these marginal areas.

Chicago's low-rent city housing projects have increased rather than decreased segregation with 85% of the tenants Negro in a 1959 survey. Most of these projects are located in predominantly Negro sections and they have not attracted low-income white families.

In contrast, several interracial housing developments such as Lake Meadows and Prairie Shores on Chicago's South Side are outstanding examples of what sound planning can achieve in middle-income integrated housing. Another illustration of successful interracial housing is the Hyde Park–Kenwood renewal project carried out under the auspices of the Community Conservation Board of Chicago with federal urban renewal aid. The cooperation of the whites living near the University of Chicago who resisted leaving when Negroes moved into the area is considered decisive in the creation of that relatively stable interracial community in the center of Chicago.

PUBLIC ACCOMMODATIONS

Illinois Negroes have made substantial gains toward free access to public and private facilities. Discrimination is prohibited in Illinois recreational and transportation facilities, as is discriminatory advertising. The public accommodations question in Illinois is intimately aligned to the overriding housing problem. In areas of the state where there is an acceptance of desegregated neighborhoods there is a corresponding tolerance of shared public accommodations. Where there is no such acceptance, there is greater discrimination in local public accommodations. Bowling alleys, lunch counters and similar facilities remain overwhelmingly segregated in Southern Illinois.

CORE concentrated on "wade-ins" to desegregate Chicago beaches during the past summer. Firm police action protected the Negro bathers and drew Attorney General Kennedy's praise.

INTERRACIAL MARRIAGE

Illinois has no law banning interracial marriage.

INDIANA

"Niggers—Don't let the sun go down on you here!"

SIGN SEEN IN A NUMBER OF COUNTY SEATS AND SMALLER COMMUNITIES IN SOUTHERN INDIANA ONLY A FEW YEARS AGO

It is well known in Indiana that Negroes are, to all practical effect, forbidden to establish residence in one-third of the state. The last survey that was taken—as long ago as 1946—indicated that there were *no* Negro voters in 30 of the southern 92 counties of Indiana.

The law has obviously been well in advance of community practices in relation to discrimination in Indiana. As in several northern states, statutes have been on the books for years forbidding discrimination in public accommodations, housing and employment in Indiana. There has been no reported enforcement.

VOTING

There appears to be no organized effort to deprive the Negro of his right to vote in Indiana. But it should be noted, in consideration of the quotation above, that it is necessary to be able to establish legal residence before registering to vote.

EDUCATION

The scarcity of public records prevent a meaningful evaluation of the actual progress of educational integration in Indiana. A report prepared by the Assistant Superintendent of the Indianapolis Public School System in 1958 showed that 24% of the students enrolled in the Indianapolis schools that year were Negro. Eighteen per cent of the teachers in the system (21% of the newly-hired) were also of that race. There were 566 Negro teachers in the Indianapolis school system in 1959, a significant increase over 1949. One hundred and fifty-nine of these teachers had affiliated with schools that previously maintained exclusively white faculties.

The Negro enrollment in higher education in Indiana is exceedingly low. The president of the Indiana State Teachers College, in analyzing this phenomenon, stated that the probable reason for it was the limited opportunities for Negro college graduates in the state. He regarded the low enrollment as particularly disquieting because Negro high school students receive desegregated education fully equal to that of whites.

All six public institutions of higher education in Indiana were able to answer a recent questionnaire about racial segregation of the student bodies in the negative.

EMPLOYMENT

The Indiana FEPC had no enforcement powers until 1960. It has been stated that most Indiana business firms do not discriminate in hiring unskilled workers, that nearly half of them hire semi-skilled workers on merit but that two-thirds of them discriminate in filling skilled jobs and nine-tenths exclude Negroes from office, sales and engineering positions. Jews, to a lesser extent, are similarly discriminated against.

Some 75 Indiana companies have recently been cooperating in a program of merit employment under the auspices of the Indianapolis Commission on Human Rights and the Association for Merit Employment, Inc. Stimulated by the local American Friends Service Committee, this program has encouraged Negro youth to train and apply for skilled jobs.

A law, called for in the Governor's Message to the Legislature, to create a State Civil Rights Commission with enforcement powers to prohibit employment discrimination, is still pending before the legislature.

HOUSING

Undoubtedly, there is almost total segregation in Indiana housing and even new housing is being built for racial groups with none scheduled on an open occupancy basis. An analysis by the Indiana Advisory Committee of the U.S. Committee on Civil Rights, focusing on the four cities of South Bend, Fort Wayne, Anderson and Indianapolis, reached the following conclusions:

1. 50 to 98% of the nonwhites in the four cities occupy substandard housing.
2. Nonwhites are almost exclusively confined to undesirable neighborhoods.
3. Minority groups fail to receive their proportional share of new housing.
4. All housing is constructed on a segregated basis.
5. No mortgages can be obtained for nonsegregated housing.
6. Real estate boards do not admit members of minority groups.

The problem of discrimination in housing in Indiana is bound to become even more acute with the continued migration of Negroes to the state in search of employment.

PUBLIC ACCOMMODATIONS

A civil rights statute of 1885 makes discrimination in public transportation because of color unlawful. No case of violation has been discovered.

Indiana's long-standing laws forbidding discrimination in hotels, restaurants and public places have been, as previously mentioned, honored in the breach. Negroes have been known to be admitted to such establishments when accompanied by whites.

INTERRACIAL MARRIAGE

Marriage between white and Negro is prohibited by law in Indiana.

IOWA

"In Sioux City Memorial Park a Winnebago Indian who had been killed in combat in Korea was refused burial after services had been conducted at the grave site and the burial party had disbanded. His widow sued for damages in an Iowa court to compensate her for the mental suffering accruing to her from the defendant cemetery's refusal to carry out the contract with her whereby the cemetery had agreed to afford the plaintiff the right of burial in a specified place. As this same contract also contained a clause stating that 'burial privileges accrue only to members of the Caucasian race,' the cemetery directors declared that this clause made it illegal for them to grant burial to the Indian as soon as they found out that he was not a member of the Caucasian race."

FROM RICE V. SIOUX CITY MEMORIAL PARK, 245 IOWA 147

Iowa courts upheld the legality of this restrictive covenant—carried to the nth degree, but later the state legislature passed a law which barred cemeteries from refusing burial because of race or color.

Another well-known discriminatory practice reported in Iowa is the refusal of the state's white barbers to cater to Negroes.

VOTING

There is little evidence of discrimination against the state's minority groups in this area. Research on the treatment of Indians and their registration procedures for voting is currently under way.

EDUCATION

Iowa laws prohibit discrimination and segregation in public schools. As the Negro population in the state is still comparatively small, the problem of segregation is relatively minor. What educational segregation there is in Iowa, exists because of the segregated housing of the large cities and towns. Iowa authorities in several communities have recently begun to express concern over this *de facto* segregation in the state's schools but despite several proposals, no concrete action has yet been taken.

EMPLOYMENT

Although Iowa was one of the first four states to pass a state Civil Rights Act (in 1884), the provisions of the statute have always been regarded as remedial in nature and, despite penal authority, it has never been interpreted strictly. Outside of this old law, Iowa has no FEPC act.

Discrimination against both Negroes and Indians is practiced in Iowa, particularly in hiring for secretarial, clerical or any positions above the unskilled level. These two minority groups also find it difficult to obtain apprenticeships for training in the various crafts. Jews in the state have met with employment discrimination in attempting to rise to management and executive levels.

The first city in Iowa to take steps toward the legal outlawing of this deprivation of equal job opportunity was Des Moines which issued a local ordinance barring discrimination in both public and private employment.

HOUSING

Most Negroes in Iowa inhabit the poorer sections of the big towns which are consequently developing into slum ghettos as the whites move out. In Mason City the situation is most acute. Negroes have no choice but to buy homes in irreparable condition; attempts to move into other neighborhoods have been met with both open and hidden white hostility. Petitions are circulated urging boycott of the Negroes and both selling and renting prices are raised exorbitantly. The Negro population is leaving Mason City because of the inability of the young people to find either employment or proper housing.

Although the housing situation is better in Des Moines, Negroes there are forced to pay higher prices than whites when buying or renting. Only a few manage to move into the better neighborhoods; the majority are relegated to unsanitary and squalid slums. In Sioux City, Marshalltown, Waterloo and Council Bluffs there is a definitely greater access to decent housing. There, Negroes who have the means can move into almost any neighborhood without fear of discrimination.

PUBLIC ACCOMMODATIONS

Iowa law guarantees to all persons "full and equal enjoyment of the accommodations, advantages, facilities and privileges of inns, restaurants, chophouses, eating houses, lunch counters and all other places where refreshments are served; public conveyances, barber shops, bath houses, theaters and all other places of amusement." Violation of the law can result in a $100 fine or 30 days in jail. As has been pointed out in the case of barber shops, the law is often more advanced than state practice.

Most restaurants in Iowa serve Negroes and many hotels accept them as guests, although the Negro is not solicited anywhere. Discrimination has been noted in swimming pools, bath houses, bowling alleys and some public parks in the state.

INTERRACIAL MARRIAGE

Iowa has no law banning interracial marriage.

KANSAS

"Because public accommodations are not extended to all citizens on an equal basis, much damage is done economically and socially. The economic factor is self-explanatory. The social damage requires some elaboration. In the case of motels refusing service, tourists are forced to become highway hazards because they cannot stop and rest when they are fatigued."

SIDNEY H. ALEXANDER, JR., EXEC. DIR., WICHITA URBAN LEAGUE

The pattern of discrimination in Kansas is confusing, erratic, and unpredictable. A Negro family traveling along a highway may be refused service by one restaurant and then be served courteously by another just a few hundred feet further up the road. This extreme unpredictability has an all-too-predictable effect on the morale of the Negro and Mexican-American population of Kansas.

Kansas, the great western border-state where the conflict between southern and northern settlers precipitated the Civil War, remains today locked between the conflicting patterns of the North and South. Liberal civil rights laws provide that there shall be no discrimination on account of race, color or previous condition of servitude in any inn, hotel, boarding house or place of amusement for which a license is required by a municipality. However, the Kansas State Supreme Court has held that restaurants and ice cream parlors do not come within these statutes.

VOTING

The U.S. Commission on Civil Rights found minor evidence of discriminatory denials of voting rights in northern and western states, including Kansas. Racial, religious or national origin statistics are not issued by Kansas.

EDUCATION

Kansas was one of three states that maintained "permissive" segregation in its public schools at the time the Supreme Court handed down the 1954 decision. A long history of school segregation under the sanction of state law had existed in Kansas since the Civil War. Eventually, through amendment and clarification, the segregation provisions had become applicable only to the grades below high school and in cities of the first class (15,000 population), except in Kansas City where segregation was expressly permitted at the high school level as well.

Kansas courts have repeatedly held that the boards of education of cities and towns of the second class did not have the authority to segregate their schools. In 1957 the provision of the Kansas code which had given cities of the first class the power to segregate was repealed by the Kansas legislature.

Actual desegregation in Kansas has developed simultaneously with the legal re-evaluations. Leavenworth achieved the goal with the parallel completion of a building expansion program. Coffeyville, on the Oklahoma border, also brought about desegregation at all levels when new school facilities became available. Topeka implemented a desegregation plan with success although the Topeka School Board had been one of the original defendants in the school segregation cases before the U.S. Supreme Court. Kansas City, Kansas, the second largest city in the state and the one with the largest Negro population, began its changeover in September, 1954, at both elementary and high school levels. CORE is still picketing *de facto* segregated schools in Kansas City.

EMPLOYMENT

There is clear evidence of widespread employment discrimination in Kansas although no bias has been reported on the basis of creed or religion. The Kansas Anti-Discrimination Act has not been instrumental in the elimination of unfair employment practices. A report to the Civil Rights Commission found that the reasons for this failure were (1) a lack of sincere cooperation on the part of some employers, including state government officials, (2) insufficient funds to permit more intensive field work and a broad community education program throughout the state, and (3) a lack of enforcement provisions.

Members of minority groups are unable to secure jobs on management levels and they must be content with unskilled employment and, in a few cases, with semi-skilled positions. Interviews with family heads of 364 families composed of 142 white, 112 Negro and 110 Mexican-Americans as well as with a cross-sectional sample of employers in Topeka revealed the following: No Negroes or Mexican-Americans held any sales positions. Over half of the white, but only one-fifth of the minority group workers made over $80 a week. Forty per cent of the white, but only 13% of the Negro workers and 14% of the Mexican-Americans earned over $2.00 an hour. Almost half of the Negroes but only one-tenth of the whites earned as little as $1.50 an hour.

The Kansas report threw some interesting light upon the often expressed contention that Negroes would have greater employment opportunities with greater educational attainments. The report found that Negroes with all or some high school education had a much harder time than whites with equivalent education in obtaining work at a par with their educational experience.

HOUSING

Practically complete segregation in all types of public and private housing is the norm for Negroes and Mexican-Americans in Kansas. Jewish citizens, on the other hand, are not confronted with discrimination in the purchase and rental of houses. The problem in Kansas is notable for not being restricted to those Negroes who cannot afford decent housing because of low income. It is actually most acute for those who are financially able to afford good and even luxury housing.

Segregation in the state appears to have increased as almost none of the newer housing developments have admitted those Negroes and Mexican-Americans who could afford them. The housing programs of the federal government have unwittingly contributed to segregation, it has been alleged, by making housing available to racial minority groups only on a segregated basis.

PUBLIC ACCOMMODATIONS

Although segregation in most public accommodations is in violation of Kansas law, the real accessibility of such facilities is, as has been noted, peculiarly random. There is definitely less discrimination in the larger cities; medium-sized and small towns persist in the perpetuation of segregation. Nevertheless even in the smaller communities changes have taken place recently. Arkansas City, for instance, now has two theaters that admit all persons. Without discernible pattern, 50% of the ice cream parlors in Topeka will serve all clients while the other half continue discrimination. The possibility of Negro boycott and "sit-in" demonstrations is regarded as potentially very effective in Kansas.

INTERRACIAL MARRIAGE

Kansas has no law banning interracial marriage.

KENTUCKY

"Kentucky has traditionally been oriented toward the Deep South, but the patterns of segregation have evolved more through custom and a way of life than by virtue of state law."

A. LEE COLEMAN, *"Desegregation of Public Schools in Kentucky"*

The Negro population of Kentucky is greatest in Louisville and in several southern counties along the Tennessee border. The counties of eastern Kentucky have very small Negro populations. In 1950, only one county in the state was more than 20% Negro.

Kentucky, as a border state, has manifested a number of often contradictory reactions to the Negro quest for fuller civil rights. On the one hand the desegregation of the Louisville school system has been described as the pluperfect ideal of such a transformation, and on the other the small towns of Clay and Sturgis made their desegregations the occasions for the release of mob violence that closed the schools.

Similarly, *My Old Kentucky Home* is a bitter or sweet lament depending upon the singer; to some Kentucky Negroes it signifies living in old but well-preserved houses that represent the best housing in the South for their race, for others it implies the usual southern substandard housing.

Kentucky best exemplifies the difference between a border state and a state of the Deep South in its relation to federal law. The state and the citizens may take their traditions and inclinations from the South but in almost every case state and local officials vigorously enforce the law, no matter how unpopular the law may be.

VOTING

Kentucky has no law barring discrimination in voter registration but at the same time no complaints of any voting discrimination have been made by the 7% Negro minority.

EDUCATION

The day the school segregation cases were decided, Governor Lawrence Wetherby announced: "Kentucky will do whatever is necessary to comply with the law." In the state's largest city, Louisville, the superintendent of its schools, Dr. Omer Carmichael and his staff moved at once into a period of intensive preparation. Developing a plan based upon the fullest community consultation, desegregation in Louisville was increased a little each year.

"What I want to call attention to particularly," Dr. Carmichael has said, "is that we didn't leave the question of segregation to the initiative of the parents. It took parents' initiative to get out of a desegregated set-up if, by residence, desegregation came." By 1959, 78% of Louisville's pupils were in biracial schools.

The experiences in Clay and Sturgis were remarkable for the lack of planning and the complete surprise by which the white community was taken by the local desegregation edicts. Mob action closed down the schools in both of the towns and they have not been opened to Negroes since.

Although Kentucky has made great progress in the state program of desegregation. One hundred and twenty-three school districts are now desegregated out of a total of 172 districts with children of both races. The University of Kentucky, desegregated since 1950, is reported as having enrolled an average of 80 Negro students each year. The University of Louisville, dating its change-over from the same time, maintains a Negro enrollment of "several hundreds." Of the five other institutions of higher learning in Kentucky, at least four have nominal desegregation.

EMPLOYMENT

Kentucky has no law barring discrimination in private employment. The state, which has industries as varied as coal mining and thoroughbred horse raising and grows a variety of crops from corn to tobacco, does have an equally wide spectrum of employment opportunities for Negroes. "Blue-collar" jobs are generally the highest to which that minority can aspire.

The Urban League of Louisville interested a number of food chains in a merit employment program in 1960 that led to the hiring of Negroes in every capacity except manager. Further, General Electric and International Harvester employed Negroes on their production lines for the first time and IBM has commenced a training program for Negroes in machine operation and accounting.

HOUSING

It is obvious to everyone in Kentucky that the amount of good housing available to Negroes is far more limited than that available to whites. Neither public nor private housing is available to the state's Negroes in any quantity.

It is next to impossible for a Negro to obtain a conventional, FHA or VA housing loan in Kentucky. The ostensible reason is income level but this seems insufficient explanation when Kentucky mortgage authorities have admitted that Negroes with a $4,000 yearly income have proved to be as good financial risks as $7,000 a year whites. Loans for home improvements in slum areas are also nonexistent. Negro housing in Kentucky is almost 100% segregated.

PUBLIC ACCOMMODATIONS

There are few local ordinances requiring segregation and almost none on a state basis. In many parts of Kentucky, public meetings and entertainment events are unsegregated. There has been desegregation on the buses of the larger cities for several years. Lexington and Louisville, among other Kentucky communities, have seen movie theaters and lunch-counters desegregated by "sit-in" efforts in the last two years.

INTERRACIAL MARRIAGE

Marriage is prohibited between white and Negro.

LOUISIANA

"New Orleans, May 5, 1961. A voter registrar appearing before the Federal Civil Rights Commission here today failed the test she uses to determine whether applicants are qualified to register. The commission heard testimony that pointed to discrimination against Negroes by the official, Mary Ethel Fox of Plaquemines Parish (County). Miss Fox denied she practiced discrimination.

"Miss Fox was asked to complete a form that includes a blank in which an applicant must list his age in years, months and days. She said that she disqualified anyone who did not answer correctly. She gave her birth date as Sept. 29, 1923, and said she was 37 years, 8 months and 2 days old today. Berl I. Bernhard, commission staff director, and Dr. John A. Hannah, Chairman, noted she was 37 years, 7 months, and 6 days old.

" 'You would have disqualified yourself, if my arithmetic is correct,' Dr. Hannah (President of Michigan State University) said."

CLAUDE SITTON, *New York Times,* MAY 6, 1961

In November, 1958, the first of a continuing stream of affidavits alleging denial of the right to vote began being received by the commission from Negro citizens of Louisiana. The complainants alleged either that they had been denied the right to register in the first place, or that having been registered, their names were removed from the rolls and that they were not allowed to register again.

VOTING

According to figures published by the secretary of state of Louisiana, there were 132,506 Negroes registered to vote in 1959 and 828,686 whites. While voting-age Negroes comprised about 30% of the total voting-age population in Louisiana, they comprised only 13% of the registered voters.

In the over two years since the receipt of the original complaint, the Civil Rights Commission and U.S. Department of Justice have attempted to deal with it and subsequent other Louisiana complaints in a variety of ways. Public hearings have been held, statistics compiled, state laws analyzed and legal action initiated. The results are best described in the commission's report:

"The history of voting in the United States shows, and the experience of this commission has confirmed, that where there is will and opportunity to discriminate against certain potential voters, ways to discriminate will be found. The burden of litigation involved in acting against each new evasion of the Constitution, county by county, and registrar by registrar, would be immense.

"If any state were to pass a law forthrightly declaring colored citizens ineligible to vote, the Supreme Court would strike it down forthwith as in flagrant violation of the Fifteenth Amendment. The trouble, however, comes not from discriminatory laws, but from the discriminatory application and administration of apparently nondiscriminatory laws.

"Against the prejudice of registrars and jurors, the U.S. Government appears under present laws to be helpless to make good the guarantees of the U.S. Constitution."

Many Negroes are still actively prevented from voting in Louisiana but the pressure for voting rights is strengthening, both from the Negro community and the federal government.

EDUCATION

Determination to resist desegregation was first expressed in Louisiana by the creation, in 1954, of a Joint Legislative Committee to draft legislation to maintain segregation. The efficacy of the various measures that resulted was short-lived. Courts proceeded to strike them down as fast as the new statutes came to appeal.

When state officials lost the capacity to halt school desegregation in Louisiana, the white citizenry found the means. Headlines and photos of screaming white mothers at the time of the 1960 semester opening showed New Orleans' reaction to the token assignment of a handful of Negro pupils to formerly all-white schools. A new tactic introduced in the New Orleans' fight was the almost total withdrawal of the white student bodies. Then the state could, in the name of minimum attendance requirements, close the school (over the protests of the school boards, in some cases) and refuse to pay teachers' salaries. The few white parents and children who did attempt to cross the mob barriers were subjected to barrages of obscenity even more intense than that which daily greeted the Negro students. Eventually at least one of these families was forced to leave New Orleans because of incessant harassment in every aspect of their life.

Several countervailing factors developed in the New Orleans situation. Local committees were formed, such as SOS (Save Our Schools), to mobilize support for keeping the schools open. A St. Louis heiress offered to provide a trust fund out of which teachers' salaries could be paid. In September, 1961, token desegregation was begun in six New Orleans elementary schools. There were no incidents. Otherwise, Louisiana education is completely segregated.

The New Orleans branch of Louisiana State University began its second year of desegregation with 2,020 students, of whom 417 were Negroes. No incidents have occurred.

EMPLOYMENT

Louisiana has no law barring discrimination in employment. Neither have unions taken any steps to end employment discrimination in the state. Local Negro leaders contended that Negroes were usually denied opportunities for training and apprenticeship and then were not hired for lack of training or experience. The New Orleans Urban League has conducted a vigorous program of research and placement with some very moderate success. The first employment of Negroes as clerk-typists at the Algiers Naval Station was one of these.

HOUSING

Louisiana has a notable amount and quality of private construction of new housing for Negroes. Of course, it is segregated and the subject of a good deal of debate among Negro leadership.

Pontchartrain Park Homes outside New Orleans is one of the largest Negro housing projects in the nation. Completed in 1955, it is a well-planned community of 1,000 homes ranging in price from $10,000 to $30,000. A large park, swimming pool, and golf course is at the center. It was built on one of New Orleans' best residential sites.

PUBLIC ACCOMMODATIONS

There is mandatory segregation in some transportation and recreational facilities. Private accommodations follow almost a total policy of segregation. The New Orleans airport has been the scene of a testing of desegregated interstate accommodations. And a major campaign is being conducted to desegregate lunch-counters. The Illinois Central railroad station in New Orleans has been desegregated as have a number of other terminals in Southern Louisiana.

INTERRACIAL MARRIAGE

Marriage is prohibited between any white or Indian person and any colored person.

MAINE

"A group of Bowdoin students, I am proud to say, have been instrumental in establishing this scholarship for any southern Negro student 'who has lost an opportunity to get a college degree because of his fight for equal rights.' The scholarship was named after John Brown Russwurm, a Bowdoin graduate in 1826 and one of the first Negroes to receive a degree in the United States. Contributing to this scholarship fund is a constructive means by which all members of the Bowdoin community can indicate their concern for this problem, and their desire to bring equality of constitutional privileges to all American citizens."

DR. JAMES S. COLES, PRESIDENT OF BOWDOIN COLLEGE,
BRUNSWICK, MAINE

Maine, with over 3,000 Negroes and nearly 2,000 Indians within the state borders, has a long record of public and private concern for the rights of minorities dating back even before 1863 when the 20th Maine saved the Union at Gettysburg.

There have been repeated reports of discriminatory practices in the state, particularly affecting Jewish visitors to Maine's tourist attractions, but in contrast to some of its New England neighbors, the state has never given either official or unofficial sanction to such action. Indeed, the 99th (1959) Maine legislature enacted an antidiscriminatory law as a direct result of press accounts of reported anti-Jewish discrimination.

VOTING

The first major revision in Maine's election laws in 131 years was before the state legislature in 1961. It is the opinion of the Maine State Advisory Committee to the U.S. Commission on Civil Rights that the new election acts offer the ultimate in protection to all Maine citizens. The Maine election laws are not being modified because of discriminatory features but because of archaic, selectmen-administered management. There is no discrimination in Maine voting practices and the city of Bangor recently changed election laws to allow absentee balloting when voting dates fall on the religious holidays of any group.

EDUCATION

There is no discrimination in Maine public education. The major issue in education in the state revolves around a measure introduced into the state legislature calling for the use of public funds to pay for the transportation of parochial school students. A move to bring the controversy to a referendum is presently in progress.

EMPLOYMENT

At least one cursory investigation of employment conditions in Maine has come to the conclusion that there are very few infringements in this area. The President of the State Federated Labor Council, AFL–CIO, has said that neither race, color nor religion are determinants in either employment or union opportunities in the state. The Maine Apprenticeship Council, with all major state agencies, employers and labor groups as members, has no racial or religious provisions, nor does it recognize such criteria.

HOUSING

Both because of its history (Maine was an important junction on the pre-Civil War underground railroad that transported runaway slaves to Canada) and the small proportion of minority population, the state has a minimum of housing discrimination or segregation. The relatively recent construction of defense installations in Maine and neighboring Portsmouth, New Hampshire, has brought considerable numbers of Negro servicemen and their families into the state. The nature of their reception has not, as yet, been fully appraised.

PUBLIC ACCOMMODATIONS

There is no question but that a number of Maine summer hotels and resort communities discriminate in refusing to accept Jewish guests. The Anti-Defamation League of B'nai Brith, in an analysis of this custom throughout the United States a few years ago, singled out the Colony Hotel in Kennebunkport particularly. As mentioned earlier, recent legislation has made such discrimination illegal. It remains to be seen both how the law is administered by state authorities and how the meaning of the law is accepted by the state's citizens.

In December, 1960, two Negro exchange students from Kenya, East Africa, were refused service late at night in a Brunswick restaurant. After resulting newspaper accounts of the incident, and with a public apology to the students by the Brunswick Chamber of Commerce, the restaurant owner explained that service was refused —not because of race—but because of the lateness of the hour.

INTERRACIAL MARRIAGE

Maine has no law banning interracial marriage.

MARYLAND

"Negroes are not members of the Baltimore Real Estate Board. That is why Negro brokers label themselves as 'realtists' rather than 'realtors.' A more accurate description that has been forced upon them might be 'realists.' "

PHILIP A. CAMPONESCHI, FORMER EXECUTIVE SECRETARY, BALTIMORE EQUAL EMPLOYMENT OPPORTUNITY COMMISSION

Although the Negroes of Maryland have acquired significant political power and they are citizens of a border state with relatively liberal antidiscriminatory protection, they must be, in every sense of Mr. Camponeschi's word, "realists," to balance their lives between the often-contradictory professions of public policy and private attitudes.

For instance, despite a claim by school authorities that all of Maryland's 23 biracial school districts were desegregated "in principle," Negroes were actually attending formerly all-white schools in only 15 school districts (Baltimore and 14 counties) at the last tabulation.

Despite significant construction of new housing units in the state, diligent research in both Baltimore and the Eastern Shore counties has revealed an unvarying pattern of Negro housing deficiency.

VOTING

In the last decade the increase of the Negro's political power in Maryland has resulted in an elimination of any deprivations of the rights of suffrage in the state.

EDUCATION

Maryland has a county-unit school system. Twenty-three county districts and the independent Baltimore City district comprise the system. Only Baltimore implemented a desegregation plan in the first school year after the Supreme Court decision. The 22 other counties that had Negro school population were bound by the ruling of the state attorney general to await the implementation decree of the U.S. Supreme Court.

In early 1961, while all 23 of the state's biracial school districts were supposed to have been desegregated, the facts bear some examination.

The desegregation plans adopted by Maryland districts were of two basic designs. Under one plan, Negro parents were permitted to apply for admission of their children to a white school if it was nearer to their residence than the Negro school. The other plan was a more direct move to eliminate the dual system. As in most other states' successful desegregation plans, it called for specified schools with established attendance areas to be opened to pupils of both races. Nineteen counties adopted the first or transfer-on-application plan and 3 the second during the next few school years.

The great difficulty with the transfer-on-application plan is, of course, that it puts the burden of desegregation on the Negro parents. In the southern Maryland area particularly, this must be done in a climate of antagonism and school board recalcitrance.

So in spite of the fact that every county in the state claims to be desegregated, the number of counties actually enrolling pupils of both races in the same schools was 14 (15 counting Baltimore). In these counties, 30.5% of Maryland's Negro school children were enrolled in schools also attended by white children. Eight counties with announced policies of desegregation had not, in fact, admitted a Negro student to a white school.

Baltimore successfully desegregated its schools in 1954–55 without strife or serious incidents. Baltimore, whose school districts had never been zoned, gave parents freedom of choice of school.

EMPLOYMENT

Maryland has no law barring discrimination in private employment.

There is unquestionably considerable employment discrimination throughout Maryland. Baltimore, which does have an Equal Employment Opportunity Commission (with significant enforcement powers), has a wide variety of modern industry and a narrow variety of Negro job opportunities. The Urban League has been forced to measure its advances in the last few years with gains such as the first licensing of Negro master plumbers in Baltimore. Mr. Philip Camponeschi, the former executive secretary of the EEOC, has opinioned that the Baltimore employment situation is unlikely to improve until the state itself forms an FEPC.

HOUSING

An investigation by the Maryland Advisory Committee to the U.S. Commission on Civil Rights led to the judgment that the Federal Government was the only agency strong enough to eradicate the slum areas where the state's Negroes are housed.

In the last 15 years, the housing inventory in Baltimore has increased by 100,000 dwelling units. During the same period, less than 1% of the new units, outside public housing, were made available for Negro occupancy.

The same over-all situation has been found to exist on Maryland's famous Eastern Shore. Only in Havre de Grace in Harford County was no segregation in Negro housing found, but here also the quality of minority housing was described as inadequate.

PUBLIC ACCOMMODATIONS

A statute requiring segregation in railroad and steamship facilities was repealed in 1951. A House bill to prohibit discrimination in places of public accommodation was introduced in the legislature in 1961. "Sit-ins" have desegregated a number of previously segregated facilities.

INTERRACIAL MARRIAGE

Marriage is prohibited between white and Negro, white and Malayan, Negro and Malayan in Maryland.

MASSACHUSETTS

"A number of communities in the southeastern summer resort section of New England have evidenced discrimination in their summer colonies or developments. In East Orleans, Massachusetts, the agent of a colony wrote: 'Owners will not allow us to rent to Jewish clients. I recommend that you get in touch with agents in Hyannis.'"

Rights, AN ANTI-DEFAMATION LEAGUE PUBLICATION: FEB. 1959

Several New England states are marked by residential "club" plans which by means of restrictive covenants and "gentlemen's agreements" discriminate against outsiders; formerly Catholics, later Jewish, and now, most virulently, Negroes and Puerto Ricans.

In Massachusetts, this practice is found, among other places, in

Winchester, Weston, Wellesley, and Needham. Individual property owners and real estate operators have successfully managed to keep these desirable suburban-home sites inaccessible to Jewish families.

VOTING

The Massachusetts Commission Against Discrimination has not received any complaints concerning denials of voting rights to any of its citizens. One can vote in Massachusetts provided the age and other minimum legal and residential requirements are fulfilled.

EDUCATION

A Fair Educational Practices Act is enforced by the Massachusetts Commission Against Discrimination. Very few cases of discrimination in the area of education have been reported and the state's record is unexcelled. Teachers are hired solely on the basis of their qualifications, regardless of race or color—and almost all schools on all levels are integrated. The Commission Against Discrimination, in 1957, adopted a by-law that the request for photographs by educational institutions before accepting prospective students was an unfair educational practice.

EMPLOYMENT

An FEPC law declaring employment without discrimination as a right and a privilege covers all commercial and business enterprises in Massachusetts with six or more employees. It forbids discrimination on the grounds of race, color, religious creed, age, ancestry or national origin, giving the Massachusetts Commission Against Discrimination a broad scope for intervention.

Massachusetts, the Cradle of Liberty and the source of much of abolitionist agitation before the Civil War, has a long history of antidiscriminatory traditions. But the tremendous exodus of so much of the state's textile and light industry to the cheaper labor areas of the South, and the consequent job-pinch, have aggravated the factors of racial preference. Now that the amazing proliferation of electronic and other highly specialized, skilled-operation industries have largely filled the state's industrial gap, the problem for minority workers is seen largely as one of acquiring sufficient technical education and skill to compete in the new, highly-paid job market.

HOUSING

Widespread discrimination in housing in Massachusetts is directed mainly against Negroes and Puerto Ricans and, to a lesser degree, Jews. The historical segregation of the Irish Catholics in Boston and other large cities has been largely eliminated by their acquisition of formidable political power in the state.

In the large cities such as Boston, Worcester and Springfield, Negroes have nowhere to move but into the older neighborhoods which have been abandoned by whites as substandard and deteriorating. This starts a hopeless cycle by which minorities are relegated to substandard quarters until these blighted neighborhoods are condemned for urban renewal projects. Unable financially to afford the rents in the new construction that goes up on his former homesite, the minority citizen is forced again to find a deteriorating home being abandoned by whites where he will live until that, too, is condemned for more new construction he cannot afford. Until a formula for making urban renewal units available to Negroes is found, the cycle will continue.

A number of significant attempts have been made by private organizations, such as the American Friends Service Committee in Cambridge and Boston, Freedom House, a civic center in Roxbury, CORE and others, to carry out "good neighbor" programs for the foundation of true interracial living.

A bill prohibiting racial or religious discrimination in public and private housing was signed in April, 1959, and even more recently Governor Volpe signed a measure authorizing revocation or suspension of real estate licenses in case of violation of the earlier law.

PUBLIC ACCOMMODATIONS

Discrimination, including segregation, is prohibited in public transportation, recreational and accommodation facilities. Discriminatory advertising is also forbidden.

Discrimination in private facilities in Massachusetts is sporadic but not totally eliminated.

INTERRACIAL MARRIAGE

Massachusetts has no law banning interracial marriage.

MICHIGAN

"We welcome good neighbors to our community without regard to the color of their skin, the manner in which they worship, or the part of the world from which they come."

A STATEMENT, SIGNED BY 900 HOME-OWNERS
IN ANN ARBOR, MICHIGAN, 1959

This statement was circulated by a small group of citizens of Ann Arbor, home of the University of Michigan, to their friends.

"We found it easier to obtain signatures than many thought it would be," they reported.

This is one of a number of ways that voluntary associations of citizens have attempted to provide leadership and education in civil rights in Michigan.

They are confronted with a formidable task.

Michigan, perhaps the most famous manufacturing state in the Union, has increased tremendously in population since the '40s and World War II. A large proportion of this increase has been, and continues to be, Negro. In 1961, one out of four persons in Detroit was a Negro.

VOTING

Michigan has neither a poll tax nor reported discrimination of any kind in voter registration. Ample opportunities are provided for registration. No record is made of race, national origin or religion.

EDUCATION

Discrimination and segregation are prohibited in the Michigan public school system. Segregation has and does result when a pattern of housing segregation is present. It has been pointed out, for example, that while Negro children make up more than 7% of the Grand Rapids school population, 91% of this total are in only four of the schools in that city. Only 33 of the 1,200 teachers in the Grand Rapids School System are Negro and the first Negro teacher assigned to a white school (in 1959) is still the only one of his race so employed.

There appears to be no discrimination in the wages or working conditions of Negro teachers in any of the school systems in the state. It is apparently a genuine concern of the school boards of the so-called "Negro schools" that the quality of teaching and equipment be equal to the best. It is equally apparent that, despite a manifest need for teachers, every Negro teacher cannot be employed in the Michigan public school systems. Particularly in Detroit where many applicants have been refused, a serious problem has developed around provisional or inadequate certification. This is the result of many Negro teachers migrating from the South. Often their educational backgrounds do not meet the standards necessary to be certified as a teacher in Michigan.

Little or no discrimination at the higher levels of education is evident in Michigan. The state universities, by charter, determine enrollment to a great extent by residential preference but, otherwise, there is a good deal of evidence that both the state and private institutions adhere to nondiscriminatory admissions.

EMPLOYMENT

As jobs in the automobile and allied industries are without a doubt the main attraction for a majority of the Negroes who migrate to Michigan from other states, it is obvious that employment must continue to be one of the most critical areas of civil rights in Michigan.

"Last hired and first fired" has been the bitter motto of Negroes for decades on their position in the employment market. It cannot be improved upon or amended for Michigan in 1961. When cars are sold and Detroit and Pontiac and Flint hum, the Negro works; at the first sign of distress he is the first to be laid off. To a degree there are a number of reasonable explanations of this, having nothing to do with discrimination. The Negro, who migrates to Michigan from the South, is almost invariably lowest in seniority and job classification. But there also seems to be an appreciable number of purely discriminatory factors involved in many cases. Neither unions, management nor the pivotal employment agencies can claim application of absolutely desegregated policy. An FEPC has been in operation in Michigan since 1955 with enforcement machinery. Yet Negroes in the automobile industry are still predominantly employed on the assembly lines with little chance of being upgraded.

HOUSING

Although there has been an amazing rise in home ownership by Negroes in Detroit (a 300% increase from 1940 to 1950), they are still largely confined to housing abandoned by white families moving to the suburbs. The pattern of segregated housing is determined both by economic and restrictive pressures. Not only Negroes, but other minority groups suffer discrimination in housing: Mexicans, Puerto Ricans and Mexican-Americans who have settled in Michigan communities can find nowhere to live but in the Negro areas or immediately adjacent to them.

The plight of the Jewish community in Detroit received national publicity last year when it was revealed that Grosse Pointe, Detroit's most desirable suburb, had a point-system for evaluating prospective home buyers that made it all but impossible for Jews to acquire property in the area. Jewish citizens are subject to housing discrimination in many areas of Michigan, particularly in suburban developments.

PUBLIC ACCOMMODATIONS

Michigan law makes it a crime to deny public accommodations to any person because of race, creed or national ancestry. Actual conditions vary in each of the state's 48 counties but there is no significant record of discrimination in this regard. Discriminatory advertising is also effectively banned. The most publicized instance of public accommodation discrimination in recent years has been at public bathing beaches.

INTERRACIAL MARRIAGE

There is no legislation pertaining to interracial marriage in Michigan.

MINNESOTA

	APPROVED	DIS-APPROVED
June 27, 1954 "Do you approve or disapprove of having white and Negro families living in the same residential districts?"	42%	49%
March 4, 1957 Same question.	44%	47%
Jan. 4, 1959 "There's been talk in Minnesota of adopting a law which would guarantee every person the legal right to buy or rent housing, regardless of his race, religion or color. Do you yourself favor or oppose having such a law?"	46%	46%
"Take the case of public housing projects where State or Federal tax money is spent. Suppose the Minnesota Legislature were asked to adopt a law which would give qualified people an equal chance to get into public housing projects, regardless of race, religion or color. Would you be for or against that kind of law?"	74%	18%

The Minnesota Poll;
PUBLIC OPINION SURVEY OF *The Minneapolis Tribune*

The extent of public acceptance of integrated housing when it is put in the reference of the average American's relation to the law has been strikingly revealed by the unique and continuing *Tribune* poll of Minnesota citizens' changing attitudes over the years. It has been pointed out how these findings challenge the view that community attitudes harden as antidiscriminatory legislation advances.

VOTING

Careful investigation has discovered no discrimination or denial of voting rights in Minnesota. This is as true among Indians as other minority groups and is corroborated by the officers of Minnesota's Chippewa Tribe.

EDUCATION

Minnesota's elementary and secondary schools are completely integrated and the formerly prevailing prejudice against the employment of nonwhite schoolteachers has been considerably reduced in recent years

The number of nonwhite students in Minnesota institutions of higher learning has risen from 601 in 1954–55 to 1,039 in 1958–59. Most private colleges have followed the lead of the public universities and colleges and shown a willingness to accept all qualified applicants regardless of race, color, religion or national origin.

Strong affirmation has been given that the Medical School of the University of Minnesota has abandoned the quota system it was allegedly following in admissions policy ten years ago.

EMPLOYMENT

Minnesota has an FEPC law which declares the right to employment to be a matter of public policy and has jurisdiction over all employers with eight or more employees. Discrimination in employment on the basis of race, creed, color or national origin is prohibited. The Minnesota FEPC has enforcement provisions.

Actual discrimination is not unknown in employment but well-established avenues of redress indubitably exercise a restraint upon such practices and serve as a harbinger of even greater opportunities for Minnesota minority groups.

HOUSING

Extensive discrimination against Negroes, Indians, and other non-whites with respect to the quality and availability of housing has been found in Minnesota. This discrimination is less marked against Jews since World War II as a consequence, probably, of the improved Jewish economic position. A five-year study of case histories revealed the following discriminatory practices:

—Deprivation of access to new housing in metropolitan areas.
—Growing concentration (segregation) of minority group families.
—Rising costs, both in purchase price and rent, to Negroes.
—Less liberal financing terms for minority groups.
—Greater prevalence of high cost secondary financing for Negroes.
—Substantially higher incidence of substandard housing for Negroes.
—Greater impact of condemnation upon minority group families.

This actual worsening minority group housing dilemma should be noted in relation to the public opinion sampling of the *Tribune*. Negroes and other minority groups are caught in a vise of housing strangulation because of economic factors at the same time that public acceptance of a more integrated way of life is evolving. On February 23, 1961, an antidiscrimination housing bill was introduced in the Minnesota legislature.

PUBLIC ACCOMMODATIONS

Discrimination and segregation are prohibited in public accommodation facilities in Minnesota. Except in a number of private clubs, this standard is well observed throughout the state.

INTERRACIAL MARRIAGE

The state has no law banning interracial marriage.

MISSISSIPPI

"The time to act is now! Throughout this nation we can end segregation in bus, train and airline terminals if we are willing to make the sacrifices involved. These are sacrifices of your time, your money and your safety. The decision to act must be made calmly and deliberately, with full knowledge of the risks and opportunities."

JAMES FARMER, DIRECTOR OF CORE
FROM THE JACKSON, MISSISSIPPI JAIL

The focus of the famous "Freedom Riders" switched dramatically in late May of 1961 from Alabama to Mississippi. A vivid contrast was immediately revealed between the responses of the two Deep South states to the nationally-publicized assault on their segregated public accommodations. Where Alabama officials lost control of their own citizens and eventually saw order restored only by the intervention of federal marshals, Mississippi circumvented that dilemma by arresting the "Freedom Riders" immediately upon their arrival at the bus terminal in Jackson. This course, however, may in the long run prove to be even more self-defeating than that of Alabama. The state arrested more than 300 visitors traveling in interracially mixed buses and CORE has pledged to continue and multiply the riders. So many of the Freedom Riders chose to serve their jail sentences that the local Jackson jail soon overflowed and the Freedom Riders have been transferred to the state penitentiary. The U.S. Attorney General has declared the right to interstate travel and terminal facilities without discrimination an interest of the federal government and Mississippi stands to lose hundreds of thousands of dollars on appeals when the hundreds of cases emerge from the state to the federal courts. Governor Ross Barnett has pledged unyielding resistance to the Freedom Riders and the outcome of this first serious challenge to the state's segregation practices in violation of federal law is yet to be determined.

VOTING

A formidable array of intimidation threatens the Negro in Mississippi who attempts to secure his citizen's right to vote. Poll taxes, refusals to accept poll taxes, complicated literacy tests and even overt danger to life and limb confront the Negro who seeks to register.

The U.S. Department of Justice filed two suits on July 6, 1961, against Forrest and Clarke counties, charging that voting rights showed a "clear-cut pattern of discrimination" against Negroes. Attorney General Robert Kennedy, in announcing the suits, stated that a majority of the 22,000 whites in Forrest County were registered but only 25 of the eligible 7,495 Negroes. In Clarke County, he said, not one of the 3,000 Negro residents is registered. Governor Barnett called the suits an invasion of local self-government.

It has been estimated that in 1955 only 4% of the eligible Negro voters were registered in Mississippi. It is also estimated that only 2% actually voted because of the number eliminated by the poll-tax qualifications. More than an estimate is not possible as state registrars have refused to comply with Civil Rights Commission requests to examine registration rolls. The filing of the Justice Department suits indicate, however, that the situation has not improved.

When attempting to register, Mississippi Negroes may be directed to write a section of the state constitution and then give a "reasonable interpretation" of it. Most Negroes are not even allowed to register, being turned away by the registrar on a number of pretexts. 98.4% of the Negroes in Mississippi who have reached voting age do not have the franchise.

EDUCATION

Seven years after the Supreme Court decision, Mississippi's schools remain completely segregated. In fact the state has gone so far as to enact an interposition resolution branding the Supreme Court decision an invasion of the process of amending the U.S. Constitution. In 1956, Mississippi created a "State Sovereignty Commission" to "resist Federal usurpation and encroachment" and repealed its compulsory school attendance law. Finally, in 1958, the state legislature authorized its governor to close public schools and other institutions of higher learning when he believed such closure would be in the interest of the state or would promote public peace and tranquillity.

There are five colleges and universities for white students in Mississippi, all of which are accredited by the Southern Association. None of the three Negro colleges is a member of the Association, although two have "qualified" approval. All of the 14 junior colleges for whites are accredited; none of the three Negro equivalents.

During the 1957–58 school year, Mississippi spent $9.08 of public funds for white higher education per white resident as compared with $1.36 for Negro higher education per Negro resident. The official educational doctrine of the state is "separate but equal."

Two attempts by Negro graduate students to enroll in Mississippi institutions of higher education have met with violent opposition. The most recent case, that of Clyde Kennard trying for the third time to register at Mississippi Southern College in September of 1959, resulted in riot, arrest and Kennard's banishment from the campus.

EMPLOYMENT

Employment discrimination is an openly-stated policy of Mississippi. When the state was negotiating a contract with the Federal Bureau of Indian Affairs in 1954, it insisted on omitting the standard nondiscrimination clause. However, the President's Committee on Government Contracts refused to permit the bureau to make the agreement with Mississippi on such terms. Mississippi has no FEPC law and refuses to cooperate with the federal government on the accumulation of employment discrimination data.

HOUSING

Mississippi Negroes live in a condition of total segregation, mostly in substandard houses and apartments. They are not allocated a proportional share of either publicly-financed housing or private construction.

PUBLIC ACCOMMODATIONS

All public accommodations throughout Mississippi follow a strict policy of complete segregation. White sentiment is so unyielding that sit-ins have not even been seriously attempted in the state. The facilities that the "Freedom Riders" were endeavoring to desegregate are under the jurisdiction of the Interstate Commerce Commission and beyond the purview of state authorities.

Mississippi's response to the nonviolent testing of its public transportation facilities has been the immediate arrest of every Freedom Rider, white or Negro, on breach of the peace charges, $200 fines, and four-month jail sentences. Jackson Negroes have countered with a local boycott which is being fiercely resisted, in turn, by the white community.

Mississippi has already lost hundreds of thousands of dollars in the jail costs of the "Freedom Riders" and stands to lose even more in court costs. The recent intervention in the case by the Justice Department as "a friend of the court" assures that the issue of desegregation of public accommodations in Mississippi will get a full legal hearing.

INTERRACIAL MARRIAGE

Mississippi law prohibits marriage between white and Negro or Mongolian.

MISSOURI

"I say they (the 'Freedom Riders') should stay home and mind their own business. Let the Courts and the Congress take care of those things."

HARRY S. TRUMAN OF INDEPENDENCE, MO.

But the Freedom Riders and the young Negroes agitating for the fulfillment of their civil rights are not staying home—even in Missouri. Free access to public accommodations is a very live issue in Missouri. Progress in antidiscriminatory measures in education, employment and housing, while still very high on minority groups' priority list, have been underscored by the grass-roots pressure for desegregation of various aspects of Missouri Negroes' daily life. And Missouri has also seen strong counterattacks against desegregation by some of the state's merchants.

A St. Louis statute that was passed in 1961 prohibiting racial discrimination in the city's places of public accommodation was challenged by six restaurants and a steamboat excursion company as violating their property rights guaranteed by the 14th Amendment. The Congress of Racial Equality has led several campaigns in St. Louis and other sections of the state for a more liberal public accommodation practice.

Thirteen incidents of anti-Jewish actions were reported to have occurred in Missouri during the December 1959–January 1960 wave of such outbreaks. The existence of a neo-Nazi youth party in two Kansas City high schools was disclosed, replete with explosives, Nazi armbands and party cards. A synagogue was bombed in Kansas City.

VOTING

At least one study has concluded that voting procedures and opportunities are available to all citizens regardless of race or creed.

EDUCATION

Little progress toward desegregation has been made in Missouri since 1958, according to the Southern Education Reporting Service. Fifty-five out of 100 school districts which reported on the subject had taken some steps by that school year but the vast majority of Negro pupils are still attending segregated schools. Even in Kansas City and St. Louis which are justly proud of their excellent desegregation records, high schools like Vashon and Sumner—and Banneker elementary school in St. Louis—remain completely segregated, primarily because of segregated housing patterns.

One result of the desegregation that has taken place in Missouri has been a decrease in Negro teachers. Many who were displaced from former all-Negro schools found it impossible to obtain jobs in mixed schools due to the prevailing bias or, in some cases, to their lack of preparation and academic requirements.

All 11 public colleges which were segregated at the time of the Supreme Court decision have since desegregated. Lincoln University, formerly entirely Negro, has a sizable white student body today. Integration on the teacher level, however, has hardly begun. Only 2 of the 11 colleges—Harris Teachers and Lincoln—currently maintain Negroes as regular members of their faculties.

EMPLOYMENT

Missouri has not yet enacted an FEPC law, although one was recently recommended by the Human Rights Commission. The Missouri State Advisory Committee to the U.S. Commission on Civil Rights has reported: "Nonwhite workers are not able to sell their labor freely on the open market. When employed, they are generally relegated to unskilled labor, domestic, or menial tasks."

Labor unions have been exceptionally inactive in Missouri in upgrading their Negro members and several Negroes have been found in occupational classifications below their trained capacities. In St. Louis the gross average income of Negro workers was only 58% of that of their local white co-workers in 1950.

HOUSING

Racial and religious discrimination in housing exists in varying degree in all sections of the state. Negroes and Jews are most affected. Negroes are restricted to the older sections of the larger cities and unable to secure housing in the suburbs. Jews are meeting difficulty in attempts to buy or rent in the "better" residential sections.

The federal government has not insisted on the inclusion of anti-discriminatory clauses in its contracts with private or public developers. Only in St. Louis is low-rent housing available to all on an open-occupancy basis. The same open-occupancy policy was adopted for one new low-rent project in Kansas City. All other projects are administered on a racially segregated pattern.

PUBLIC ACCOMMODATIONS

Many Missouri hotels, restaurants, cafeterias, motels and theaters are still closed to Negroes. In St. Louis, Kansas City, Jefferson City, Columbia and other places, Negroes are accommodated in many hotels and visit local "white" theaters.

Most recreational facilities such as bowling alleys, skating rinks, swimming pools and golf courses are operated on a strictly segregated basis.

INTERRACIAL MARRIAGE

Missouri prohibits marriage between white and Negro or Mongolian.

MONTANA

"Excepting for the Indians, the great majority of whom live on reservations, we do not have people who are generally classed as a minority group. As you know, there are very few people of the Negro or Oriental races in Montana. In fact, you could almost say that all our people are of the Caucasian race."

HARRY O. DUELL, DIRECTOR,
MONTANA FEDERAL HOUSING ADMINISTRATION

There are seven major Indian tribes in Montana; the Blackfeet, Crow, Fort Belknap, North Cheyenne, Fort Peck, Flathead and the Landless Indians, Incorporated. They are loosely affiliated for purposes of dealing with federal and state officials into an Intertribal Policy Board.

Among the comments made by representatives of Montana's tribes to the State Advisory Committee to the U.S. Commission on

Civil Rights, the most heavily stressed was the tribes' complaint of the excessive "paternalism" of the Federal Bureau of Indian Affairs.

Montana, as a major farming state, also has a large influx of migratory labor every summer. Predominantly Mexican-American, these workers come from Texas and Arizona for the two-month harvesting season. It has been stated by the chairman of the Unemployment Compensation Commission of Montana that there have been no cases wherein the civil rights of these workers have been violated.

VOTING

There has been no reported discrimination in voting or registration in Montana.

EDUCATION

Montana has never had any segregation in its public school system except for the Indian schools on the reservations. The standard of education in these schools, however, is regarded as comparable to the state's. Migrant children have usually finished their school terms by the time they enter Montana.

EMPLOYMENT

Indians have not objected to employment practices in Montana except where federal or state work has been done on the reservations and tribal members have been excluded from the projects. The Intertribal Council has pointed out that local intimidation has often accompanied the administration of unemployment compensation benefits.

The employment conditions of Montana's seasonal workers are the same as those of other migratory laborers. Not covered by minimum wage laws, they generally are hired at substandard pay rates.

Recommendations that have been made for the alleviation of the migrants' plight include remuneration for travel from point of hire, occupational and other insurance coverage, piece-work rates at least equal to those set by the U.S. Department of Agriculture, the right to negotiate rates for particularly difficult work and a minimum hourly wage if the piece rate is inadequate and unfair.

HOUSING

Some 95% of the housing units provided for migrants in Montana have been inspected. Excellent cooperation from most farmers in bringing their establishments up to minimum standards has been reported by the state.

There is no serious housing segregation in Montana except in the case of native Indians who when they leave the reservations find it impossible to secure adequate housing. The root reason is that they are unable to obtain mortgages.

PUBLIC ACCOMMODATIONS

Indians are unable to secure service in many areas. If temporarily absent from their reservations they are frequently denied hospitalization or medical treatment.

INTERRACIAL MARRIAGE

A Montana law banning interracial marriage was repealed in 1953.

NEBRASKA

"What better moral right have thirty-one citizens of Nebraska to say that the thirty-second shall not hold slaves, than the people of thirty-one states have to say that slavery shall not go into the thirty-second state at all?"

ABRAHAM LINCOLN IN A SPEECH ON OCTOBER 16, 1854, PEORIA, ILLINOIS

Nebraska was the center of civil rights controversy even before it was a state; even before it was a territory or, indeed, settled. It was the debate over the Kansas–Nebraska Act in 1854 that started

Abraham Lincoln on his national political career and Stephen A. Douglas on his national political decline.

Actually, of course, Nebraska came to be settled by the staunchest of "free-soilers" and never had a significant Negro minority until recent years when the state became more industrialized.

Perhaps the most critical of these minority problems in Nebraska is in the area of housing. But unlike many states, in Nebraska the housing situation isn't only confined to the cities. As early as 1954 a governor's committee stated: "We have even discovered that farmers of minority races find it difficult to buy land on which to farm." Also: "In the cities racial minorities face residential segregation in its most rigid form, and it is buttressed and supported by restrictive covenants."

VOTING

There is no evidence of discriminatory voting practices against Negroes in Nebraska. Some instances have been reported in relation to the Indian and Mexican-American minorities but because there is a language and English literacy factor present here, it has been difficult to determine the actual degree of discrimination.

EDUCATION

At no time has there been any discrimination in Nebraska schools on the basis of color, creed, race or religion. Public elementary and secondary schools do not even keep records of race or religion, nor do the state-supported colleges.

State law assures that teachers applying for jobs are not questioned about their religion. No segregation of any variety is present in Nebraska schools.

EMPLOYMENT

Nebraska has no statutory prohibition against discrimination in employment and except for federally-administered defense work, actual employment discrimination is the practice throughout the state.

The Urban League of Omaha lately concluded a long and successful campaign to persuade city officials to integrate the fire department and institute merit hiring in the city civil service system.

HOUSING

There is no doubt that discrimination contributes, often crucially, to the substandard housing of Nebraska's Indians, Negroes, Mexicans and Orientals. In Omaha, 50% of the Negroes and 90% of the Indians live, it has been reckoned, in inadequate housing. This general ratio is about the same in Lincoln, the other major population center of the state.

Negroes have shared hardly at all in the new housing that has been constructed in the state during the last few years. Before that a number of builders had developed special projects for Negro home-owners. Around 1949, some 40-odd homes in the $8,000 to $15,000 range were built in Omaha for Negroes. The aggregate total of Omaha rental units available to Negroes in federal housing projects is 1,784.

In Lincoln the housing picture is practically the same. Older houses in Lincoln are usually the only ones available to Negroes. Discrimination is directly responsible for this as has been illustrated in reported cases where money paid in advance for apartments was returned by the landlord because the other tenants protested.

The Nebraska Advisory Committee to the U.S. Commission on Civil Rights has filed the opinion that only the federal government has attempted to do anything effective toward alleviating the minority housing situation in Nebraska.

PUBLIC ACCOMMODATIONS

A bill has been introduced in the state legislature that would add "motels, trailer courts and taverns" to the list of places of public accommodation subject to the state civil rights statute. It would also increase penalties for violations from the $100.00 present maximum to $200.00 for a second offense and to $500.00 for a third offense.

INTERRACIAL MARRIAGE

Marriage is prohibited between white and Negro, Chinese or Japanese.

NEVADA

"Negroes even have to pay a higher price for going broke in this country. By denying them the civil right to lose their shirts in our better legal and illegal gaming rooms, we are not discriminating away the mania for moola that seems to lurk in every American breast. We are simply driving Negroes with the fever into the racket-ridden 'numbers.' The odds in that little short-cut to prosperity, of course, are even longer than those we white Protestants buck at the 'slots.' "

VAL COLEMAN IN A SPEECH: *The Color of the Law of Probability*

There are only two major centers of population in the state of Nevada, Las Vegas and Reno. Their major industries are well-known. The two cities, one in the north of the state and the other in the south, are also the only two areas in the state where the denial of civil rights is common practice. There is little or no discrimination against minority groups in the other, sparsely-settled sections of Nevada.

None of the luxury-type gambling establishments of Nevada welcome Negroes or Indians to leave their savings in the state. Very few of the middle-class emporiums do either. Direct refusal to accommodate minority groups is usually avoided but their patronage is quietly discouraged. Similarly, hotels and motels in the vicinity of both Las Vegas and Reno do not accept Negro guests. Letters to each of 116 hotels and motels listed in the Reno phone book elicited only four "yeses" to the question "Do you accept Negroes as guests?" Both Reno and Las Vegas have one segregated section on the fringe of the main business areas where minority groups are granted access to public accommodations, including the "slots."

The problem of the Indian is particularly acute in Nevada. The state has been the pace-setter in the condemnation of Indian lands and the infringement of government treaties. "Squatting" by whites on valuable Indian properties has been recognized as a means of acquisition.

VOTING

Nevada has no legal discriminatory limitations on the right to vote. Indians have frequently cited instances of deprivation in the past but with their assumption of competent counsel this has ceased.

EDUCATION

Because of the small number of Negroes living in the state, discrimination in education has never been a root problem in Nevada. Educational segregation certainly exists but this is primarily because of housing segregation. Las Vegas, for example, has integrated its junior and senior high schools but the segregated residential pattern effectively maintains segregated elementary schools.

The facilities for Indian education in Nevada are inadequate throughout the state. They are almost totally segregated. Because constant agitation has always centered around the Indians' federally-bestowed lands in Nevada, mutual hostility has precluded any joint attack upon the problem of Indian illiteracy. All efforts in this direction have come from the U.S. Government.

EMPLOYMENT

It is very difficult to determine the extent of discrimination in employment in Nevada. It is generally conceded to exist but measurement is not practical because of the peculiar nature of the state's economy. Limited job opportunities for all citizens dictate, inevitably, that the Negroes and other minority groups will be on the bottom of the employment ladder.

HOUSING

Las Vegas, which contains a 20% nonwhite population, is completely segregated. It is not a conspiracy but "a matter of custom," the Nevada State Advisory Committee to the U.S. Commission on Civil Rights reports. Some 55% of the housing occupied by the minority is substandard while only 22% of that of the majority is so classified. The rate of construction for nonwhites is substantially below that for whites. Home financing for nonwhites is difficult to obtain; there are 70 real estate firms in the area; only one will act as a broker for nonwhites.

Throughout the whole state it is estimated that in most counties, 40 to 100% of the minority citizens live in substandard housing—the Indians, the state's largest minority—usually in a one- or two-room cabin without a bathroom.

Reno minority groups overwhelmingly live in segregated collections of substandard houses. Urban renewal is in the planning stages. There are 150 units of public housing now under construction in Reno that will be nonsegregated.

PUBLIC ACCOMMODATIONS

Nevada has no law prohibiting or requiring discrimination or segregation by private enterprises.

One factor which may modify the desegregation of public accommodations in the state is the imminent construction, in both Las Vegas and Reno, of multimillion dollar convention facilities. If the experience of other states with this type of operation is any guide, Nevada will be under great pressure from the business and professional societies that use these facilities to change their discriminatory customs. The managements of luxury hotels in the Las Vegas area have already indicated that they will accept future Negro guests when they are delegates to conventions at the new civic center.

INTERRACIAL MARRIAGE

A State law prohibiting marriage between Caucasian and Ethiopian, Malayan or Mongolian was repealed on April 20, 1959.

NEW HAMPSHIRE

"I think it is only fair to tell you that our clientele is largely Christian."

FROM A NEW HAMPSHIRE RESORT BROCHURE

The principal problem of civil rights in New Hampshire remains the considerable discrimination that is practiced in public accommodations in the state. The chief victims of this discrimination remain Jews and Negroes. Convincing evidence indicates that over 50% of the hotels, motels and restaurants in the White Mountains, the Lakes region and the seacoast near Portsmouth discriminate both in their advertising and their hospitality to Jews and Negroes. The traveling Negro is even less welcome than the traveling Jew. As one Negro stated: "We are the lowest on the totem pole."

At the time of the 1950 census there were only 731 Negroes and a small number of Jews living in the state out of a total population of 533,242. Approximately 40% of the Negroes lived in the Portsmouth area.

VOTING

There has never been any evidence of interference with voting rights in New Hampshire because of race, creed or color.

EDUCATION

Negro children are completely integrated within the New Hampshire school system and the five higher educational institutions of the state are among the nation's most liberal in their nondiscriminatory admissions policies.

EMPLOYMENT

It is believed that a certain amount of discriminatory practices in employment have occurred but all sections of the New Hampshire community testify to the real and forceful role the labor organizations of the state have taken to eliminate these practices. The number of Negro teachers employed by the State Board of Education is proportional to population.

HOUSING

Segregated housing, as it often exists in metropolitan areas, is not found in New Hampshire. Outside of resort regions, free choice of housing is generally available to Jews. It is recognized, however, that justifiable prudence and caution have led Jews NOT to move to the so-called "select neighborhoods." Urban renewal projects under FHA have been carried out in three New Hampshire cities, Manchester, Nashua and Portsmouth, with a notable lack of discrimination in both property assessment and relocation.

Until the opening of the large Pease Air Force Base outside Portsmouth several years ago, the housing situation of the Negro minority in that city was also relatively desegregated and adequate, if not satisfactory. Or as it has been said another way: "Occupation of substandard housing (was) . . . not confined to any one or two racial or minority groups."

The activation of the Pease Air Base brought a number of new Negro servicemen and their families to the city, an acute housing shortage and a definite increase in the reality of discriminatory housing. It has become extremely difficult for these service families to find any but slum housing and, as it was wryly remarked in a letter to the Portsmouth *Herald,* "It generally doesn't make any difference whether the landlord is Protestant, Catholic, or Jewish. It would still be, 'I'm sorry.' " In 1960 New Hampshire enacted a strong antidiscrimination housing measure.

PUBLIC ACCOMMODATIONS

It should be noted that a New Hampshire statute (RSA 354, ss.2) prohibiting a proprietor from advertising that he discriminates has been on the books for several years. It has demonstrably not prevented the practice. Summer hotel owners and managers claim the practice is forced upon them by the attitudes of their guests. Indicative of these attitudes is the response one proprietor received to a questionnaire he submitted to his regular clientele about discrimination; "92% stated that they would not return if we endeavored to cater to all segments of society." This proprietor and others have recently established a quota for minority-group guests.

Only minor evidence of this discrimination has been found in the hotels and other public and commercial accommodations in the cities and regions of New Hampshire not dependent on the resort business.

INTERRACIAL MARRIAGE

New Hampshire has no law prohibiting interracial marriage.

NEW JERSEY

"If segregated neighborhoods make the concept of the neighborhood school an instrument of segregated education, then the neighborhood school must not take precedence over the establishment of equal educational opportunities. The NAACP expresses its firm position that there can be no equality of educational opportunities with a segment of the school population attending schools either all-white or all-Negro."

MRS. JOHN SPRUILL, SEC. OF BERGEN COUNTY BRANCH, NAACP

The Lincoln elementary school in Englewood, N.J., is located in the Fourth Ward where most of Englewood's Negroes live. It accommodates 545 pupils, ten of whom are white. The local board of education has been discussing the Lincoln school problem for seven years but as yet no actual steps have been taken to alter the racial imbalance. It has been charged, in a complaint filed with the New Jersey Division Against Discrimination, that the local board of education established school districts in such a way as to exclude Negroes from particular schools and confine them to segregated schools. In 1955 the State Commissioner of Education directed the board to redraw the boundary lines so as to achieve a more equitable ratio between Negroes and whites in all the schools of the district. Subsequently, a junior high school with a practically 100% Negro enrollment was closed and the students transferred to junior highs with full desegregation. But the condition of the Lincoln elementary school is still *de facto* segregation.

VOTING

No instances of discrimination in the registration and voting practices have come to the attention of the authorities in New Jersey.

EDUCATION

The revised New Jersey State Constitution of 1947 contains a provision declaring that it is a civil right of any citizen not to be exposed to segregation in the militia or in the public schools because of religious principles, race, color, ancestry or national origin. Since that date progress in the elimination of discrimination and segregation in New Jersey public education has been considerable. Several all-Negro schools still exist in some towns due to the segregated living patterns and—as in the case of Englewood—remain the subject of controversy.

New Jersey law requires that children attend the schools closest to their homes. At the same time the state requires that school districts draw their boundaries to best maintain balanced racial enrollment. Obviously these two requirements can only be reconciled when the dispersal of minority groups is complete enough to preclude segregated housing patterns.

The State University at Rutgers is fully integrated and, since 1960, fraternities and sororities practicing racial or religious discrimination have not been allowed to maintain chapters on the campus. Four of the six state colleges have Negroes on their faculties.

EMPLOYMENT

The New Jersey Division Against Discrimination received 1,664 complaints of discriminatory practices between 1945 and 1957. This was only surpassed nationally by the number of complaints filed in New York.

New Jersey Negroes meet with discrimination in promotion to higher job classifications and Jews in the state often are prevented from obtaining positions in banking and insurance and certain other executive jobs. D.A.D. has successfully handled many of these charges by negotiation. Nevertheless, Governor Meyner has called for various improvements in the state reconciliation machinery.

HOUSING

New Jersey is the fourth smallest state in the union and with five million people the eighth most populous. It ranks seventh in the nation in federal-aid housing programs. Most of the federally-aided housing projects are integrated with Negroes constituting 20–40% of occupancy.

The private housing available to racial minority groups is steadily narrowing in New Jersey. They are compelled to rent or buy substandard housing at inflated prices and landlords, by and large, have consistently refused to make necessary repairs or provide adequate maintenance. Newark has established a City Housing Court where both tenants and public officials can summon landlords into court.

After prolonged litigation, the builders of Levittown and of Green Fields, respectively, were finally enjoined to abandon their openly discriminatory practices against Negro home-buyers. They are now required to sell to any prospective buyer who fulfills the financial qualifications.

A bill is currently pending before the New Jersey legislature which would extend the existing ban against discrimination in public and publicly-assisted housing to all housing except the owner-occupied one- and two-family rentals.

PUBLIC ACCOMMODATIONS

The New Jersey Division on Civil Rights was reorganized by a 1949 amendatory act into two sections. One continued to deal with complaints of discrimination in employment while the second section was charged to cope with "unlawful acts of discrimination." The definition of "place of public accommodation" in the amendment is so explicit and effective in enumerating all the possible techniques of discrimination that the law has become a model for other states writing antidiscriminatory legislation.

The first case of discrimination in public accommodations which could not be settled by means of conciliation was that of the Hightstown Swimming Pool which refused to admit Negroes, contending that it was a private organization not covered by the law. It was subsequently proved that whites were admitted merely on payment of the regular admission fee and the owner of the pool was ordered to open the pool to members of all races. As illustrated in the Hightstown example, New Jersey authorities appear to be determined to aggressively enforce the state's antidiscrimination laws.

INTERRACIAL MARRIAGE

New Jersey has no law banning interracial marriage.

NEW MEXICO

"The Negro population of the Albuquerque metropolitan area, including military personnel not living within the boundaries of the military reservations, is estimated at 5,500 to 6,000, or roughly 3 percent of the area's total population. By actual count the number of new housing units that have been made available to Negroes in Albuquerque on an open-occupany or first purchase basis is 24 units. This means that 0.008 percent of the new housing built has been actually available to prospective Negro purchasers."

NEW MEXICO ADVISORY COMMITTEE TO THE
U.S. COMMISSION ON CIVIL RIGHTS

New Mexico Negroes who can afford better housing automatically become the victims of real estate dealers and agents. Homes in an all-white, low-cost area which had been sold to whites after construction for $5,500 to $6,500 with an FHA down payment of $350 to $500 were found to be resold to Negroes at $7,500 to $9,000, with down payments of $750 to $1,000. These terms would have been sufficient to purchase an $8,000 to $10,000 FHA-financed home in a better area. These "better" neighborhoods, however, are not accessible to Negroes. Efforts to solve the Albuquerque housing situation in cooperation with home builders and realtors have met with failure. Realtors who vary from the prevailing practices suffer expulsion from the Realtors Association, losing the advantages of multiple listings.

New Mexico, with a total population of over 700,000, contains 6½% Indians, 2% Negroes and less than ½% Jews. Almost a third of the total population have Spanish surnames.

VOTING

Until 1950, Indians who paid no ad valorem tax were not permitted to vote in New Mexico. Since that year they have been able to exercise their elective franchise freely.

Tribal chiefs in several of the pueblos in central New Mexico have often discouraged participation in elections. However, on the important Navajo Reservation in northern New Mexico both national political parties have succeeded in recruiting Indian voters. Navajos who are unable to read or write are permitted to affix their thumbprints to their registration cards instead of their signatures.

There is no discrimination because of race, color or creed in voting, New Mexico minority groups affirm.

EDUCATION

Discrimination in education has not been acute in New Mexico. Before 1954, eight communities maintained segregated schools. Most had been desegregated by 1954. Only Clovis and Hobbs did not begin the process until after the Supreme Court decision. In Clovis the transition proceeded without incident. Hobbs was the scene of violence in the form of a dynamite blast that wrecked a classroom. Now virtually all of the schools in the state are integrated.

Indian children in the Gallup administrative area of the Bureau of Indian Affairs usually attend public schools on the reservation. A movement underway to integrate these schools into the state system is about a third completed.

EMPLOYMENT

New Mexico established an FEPC Commission in 1949. Employment without discrimination was declared a civil right and employers of four or more were placed under the jurisdiction of the law. As there was evidence of continuing discrimination in New Mexico employment practices, the state, in 1959, strengthened the FEPC law by the addition of criminal penalties for discrimination by public agencies. In 1960, the FEPC held that an employer may not prohibit the speaking of a foreign language on the job.

HOUSING

To remedy the generally acknowledged scarcity of housing for minority groups, the State of New Mexico has passed enabling legislation which authorizes municipalities to proceed with public housing programs. The only city that has utilized this authority thus far is Clovis where a completely integrated, well-administered housing facility exists.

In addition to Albuquerque, mentioned previously, Alamagordo and Farmington are cities where Negroes cannot buy property and where there are segregated trailer courts. In Carlsbad, integrated housing has reduced the magnitude of the problem to a degree and in Gallup no serious housing gap is said to remain.

PUBLIC ACCOMMODATIONS

Negroes cannot obtain rooming or hotel accommodations in the cities of Farmington, Hobbs, and Truth and Consequences. Since 1952, Albuquerque has had an ordinance banning racial discrimination in places of public accommodation, resort or amusement. Santa Fe adopted a similar provision recently.

INTERRACIAL MARRIAGE

New Mexico has no law banning interracial marriage.

NEW YORK

"The projects in Harlem are hated. They are hated almost as much as policemen, and this is saying a great deal. And they are hated for the same reason: both reveal, unbearably, the real attitude of the white world, no matter how many liberal speeches are made, no matter how many lofty editorials are written, no matter how many civil rights commissions are set up."

JAMES BALDWIN, FIFTH AVENUE UPTOWN, *Nobody Knows My Name*

Harlem is the site of the highest density of Negroes in the United States. During the last ten years Puerto Ricans also have moved, in significant numbers, into America's most famous ghetto.

New York State and New York City have traditionally been progenitors in the assurance of equal rights to minority groups. The state has pioneered in outlawing discrimination in public and private housing. New York City has gone even farther in passing antidiscriminatory legislation in every area of civil rights. It is also unquestionable that the city and the state have benefited by being the home of countless national civil rights organizations. A more than usually vigilant press has continued to focus attention on discriminatory patterns and has kept up unremitting pressure to have them liberalized.

Despite this history and these many advantages, it is fair to say that New York State, in 1961, was in the grip of a civil rights crisis in housing, education and employment more severe than any for decades. The reality of New York life for most Negroes and Puerto Ricans is the ghetto of Harlem.

VOTING

There has been no discrimination in New York voting practices for many years.

EDUCATION

De facto segregated schools is becoming an increasingly formidable problem in many of the cities of New York State. In New York City it has already reached alarming dimensions. At the time of the Supreme Court decision, there were 42 *de facto* segregated elementary and nine junior high schools in Manhattan. Today, there are 72 elementary and 12 junior highs with greater than 85% Negro and Puerto Rican student bodies. In Brooklyn in 1954, there were only nine segregated elementary schools; now there are 25.

It is a matter of dispute where the responsibility for New York City's *de facto* segregation lies. Certainly the fact that over a third of New York's public school population is Negro or Puerto Rican is fundamental to the entire problem. The segregated housing pattern that has developed in the city as a result of the tremendous minority population growth has resulted in both an over-all shortage of schools and a concentration of Negroes and Puerto Ricans in a few overburdened schools.

The City of New York has repeatedly pledged itself to end the *de facto* segregation but what progress has been made has been outstripped by the progress of segregation. New York's school board, which has been recently removed for general ineffectuality, had not been notably imaginative in facing the issue. Increasingly, the same pattern is developing in other cities of the state.

Efforts of Negro parents to transfer their children out of the overcrowded segregated schools have met with all kinds of opposition. Most recently illustrative of the elaborate obstacles put in the path of these efforts is the continuing story of suburban New Rochelle's determination to keep the town's Lincoln School segregated. The local school board most recently appealed to the U.S. Court of Appeals to set aside a Federal District Court order to desegregate the school by fall of 1961.

EMPLOYMENT

Although discrimination because of race, religion or color is prohibited in New York State by law and an FEPC with strong powers is present to enforce its provisions, job opportunities for Negroes and Puerto Ricans are stringently limited in the state.

The garment industry in New York City has seen its historical cadre of Jewish piece-workers almost completely replaced during the last ten years by newly-arriving Puerto Ricans. Negroes and Puerto Ricans perform almost all of the service occupations of the city. Considerable progress has been made in New York and other cities in the last few years in incorporating Negroes into clerical, secretarial and sales positions but managerial and executive posts are held by only a few.

Numerous instances of discrimination are reported in the New York papers. A random listing indicates that companies, unions and private employers all discriminate at various times. The New York State Commission Against Discrimination (SCAD) has even publicized job bias against Negro elevator operators.

HOUSING

Despite perceptible advances toward its alleviation through recent legislation at the state and local levels, housing discrimination remains a serious problem in New York. This segregation is a potent force in perpetuating *de facto* school segregation.

Negroes are the principal victims of housing discrimination in New York City. Puerto Ricans are also deeply affected although they live more widely outside of Harlem, primarily because the Harlem area is already so congested. Both minority groups are forced to pay more rent than whites for apartments that are less adequate. New construction has played a negligible role in meeting the housing needs of Negro and Puerto Rican families. In a recent period only 12,000 nonwhite families acquired new dwellings out of 737,000 new units built.

It should be noted that compliance with the laws banning discrimination in New York State is observed in countless instances. Many white residents have been happy to welcome Negro neighbors. But the housing industry, as reported as late as August 20, 1961 by the *New York Times,* remains reluctant to abandon existing patterns of discrimination which, it says, reflects majority public opinion.

PUBLIC ACCOMMODATIONS

Even public accommodations have become an arena for minority group clamor in New York although the state has a whole series of statutes which forbid discrimination in public places. The incident of the Forest Hills Tennis Club denying admission to the son of the U.N.'s Ralph Bunche drew national scrutiny because of the quasi-public nature of the club.

INTERRACIAL MARRIAGE

New York has no law banning interracial marriage.

NORTH CAROLINA

"The white and colored militia shall be separately enrolled, and shall never be compelled to serve in the same organization. No organization of colored troops shall be permitted where white troops are available, and while permitted to be organized, colored troops shall be under command of white officers."

STATUTORY PROVISION #127–6; NORTH CAROLINA STATE CONSTITUTION

North Carolina presents an interesting but little-known aspect of segregation in the composition of the state National Guard. The North Carolina Advisory Committee to the U.S. Commission on Civil Rights reported that as of June 30, 1959, there were 11,345 white persons enrolled in the Guard and not one Negro.

If Negroes were allowed in the Guard at the ratio of their population in the state, they would constitute 25% of the whole. This would direct, it has been estimated, about $1,350,683 in Guard pay into the Negro community. As over 96% of the money supporting the National Guard is contributed by the federal government, this North Carolina practice is regarded as directly discriminatory. Negroes are also deprived of the many real advantages accruing to an inductee to the regular National Armed Forces with prior experience in a National Guard.

North Carolina, sometimes referred to as the most liberal of the southern states, maintains segregation in most areas of everyday life.

VOTING

No official county-by-county racial voting statistics are available for North Carolina where voting discrimination is admittedly prevalent. The boards of elections in 36 of the state's 100 counties reported a substantial increase in Negro registration in 1958 over 1956, while in ten counties there was a small decline.

The voting problem in North Carolina appears to be largely that of varying practices in administering the state's literacy requirement. Would-be voters must be able to "read and write" any section of the constitution to the satisfaction of the registrar, who may have the applicant copy indicated sections or may dictate any section he chooses.

The Southern Regional Council has reported that under this broad discretion, in which a Negro's ability to vote depends on the individual registrar's sense of justice, "Negroes may find it almost impossible to qualify in one county and comparatively easy in the next."

EDUCATION

At the time of the 1954 decision of the Supreme Court, North Carolina state law dictated almost total educational segregation. The exception was the University of North Carolina which had admitted Negroes to its graduate school in 1951 as a result of litigation. Duke University, Mars Hill College and Davidson College are private institutions of higher learning that scheduled desegregation for the fall of 1961.

No actual desegregation took place in any of the state's 172 school districts (all biracial) until 1957. Two attempts to register Negro children in all-white schools in 1955 had been unsuccessful. However, the University of North Carolina did enroll Negro undergraduate students the same year—the first white public college in the South to do so.

In Greensboro, Charlotte and Winston-Salem token desegregation began with the admission of six Negro pupils to all-white public schools in 1957. John Kasper visited the state at this time and organized antidesegregation groups which later merged with local Ku Klux Klans to oppose these efforts, but state action prevented serious outbreaks of violence.

Today, token desegregation, continuing in Charlotte, Greensboro, and Winston-Salem, has been extended to Durham, Goldsboro, Havelock and High Point, making a total of seven districts out of 174 that have begun the process. Asheville has announced a desegregation policy for the first three grades. Five Negro children have been accepted.

EMPLOYMENT

Complete employment discrimination in North Carolina contributes significantly to the low income of the Negro minority. In 1950 the median family income was $2,150 for whites and $1,050 for Negroes.

HOUSING

The State Advisory Committee to the U.S. Commission on Civil Rights has observed: ". . . data indicates that low incomes and limited purchasing power of the nonwhite population are probably not the only factors which account for the abnormally high proportion of inferior housing owned or occupied by them." In other words, discriminatory traditions in North Carolina remain potent and primary.

PUBLIC ACCOMMODATIONS

Greensboro, North Carolina, was the scene of first "sit-in" protest against public accommodation segregation that swept the South in 1960. Local students sat at a lunch counter until they were carried away. Subsequent nonviolent demonstrations by Negroes have compromised a number of the segregation policies in both public and private facilities throughout the state. Until recent "Freedom Rides," segregation was mandatory in transportation by state law.

INTERRACIAL MARRIAGE

Marriage is prohibited between white and Negro, white and Indian, and Negro and Indian in North Carolina.

NORTH DAKOTA

"The Indian problem is complicated by the four points of view; the tribal view, the sympathetic 'poor Indian' view, the Park Service view, and the Indian Bureau point of view. Possibly there is evidence of racial discrimination in reverse. That is, the Indian is sometimes treated like a child, and he gets more sympathy than members of any other racial group."

JOHN HART, EXECUTIVE DIRECTOR,
NORTH DAKOTA INDIAN AFFAIRS COMMISSION

North Dakota does not have a large Negro minority but does have a considerable Indian population. There are altogether about 14,-500 Indians in the state; 9,000 living on reservations and 5,500 scattered elsewhere.

It appeared to the North Dakota State Advisory Committee to the U.S. Commission on Civil Rights, which acknowledged it was able to give the Indian problem only a limited analysis, that the condition of the Indian in North Dakota was less a question of civil rights than one resulting from conflicts "involving state and federal laws and tribal laws and customs."

There is no doubt that the condition of the Indians in the state, whatever the reason, is unfortunate. State aid to dependent children is 14 times greater for Indians than for others in North Dakota and in one county it is 48 times as great for Indians as for all other children.

VOTING

It is claimed that no Indians have suffered infringement of their rights to vote in North Dakota. The lack of Indian registration in some areas of the state is attributed to educational deficiencies. In other areas it is said that Indian voters actually maintain the balance of local political power.

EDUCATION

A survey has shown that there is no discrimination in North Dakota public schools, nor in the state institutions of higher learning on the basis of race, religion or social status. Students are accepted for admission on a standard of equality. Facilities are also equal between the public schools and the Indian schools.

EMPLOYMENT

North Dakota, with no law barring discrimination in employment, is an important agricultural state with minimal industrial employment opportunities. Nevertheless, the state has been the scene of a small but significant experiment in providing modern employment "where human dignity is preserved" for Indians. This is at the jewel plant in Rolla in the Turtle Mountains. Otherwise, the Indians of North Dakota primarily work at harvesting.

HOUSING

Indians are segregated on reservations and off the reservation in North Dakota when they reside in the white community. Overwhelmingly, this appears to be primarily an economic problem. Indian income is so low and marginal that they are not even in a position to consider any housing except substandard. No doubt discrimination in employment fortifies the perpetuation of this condition.

PUBLIC ACCOMMODATIONS

There is no North Dakota law prohibiting or requiring discrimination or segregation by private enterprises. There is a well-known catalogue of public and private establishments barred to Indians, Negroes and Orientals in the state.

INTERRACIAL MARRIAGE

A state statute banning interracial marriage was repealed in 1955.

OHIO

"In Columbus we heard from a Negro who tried to obtain financing from 13 institutions. In each case he was told 'No, the house is located in a controversial area.' It was the conclusion of the Columbus Urban League that Negro buyers, regardless of affluence, education or credit rating, would be refused and discouraged if they should attempt to purchase a home in the new developments which cater to the white market."

FROM THE REPORT ON A HOUSING STUDY MADE
BY THE OHIO CIVIL RIGHTS COMMISSION IN 1958

The assumption that real estate values in any neighborhood immediately plummet as soon as Negroes move into it has been called into serious question by certain evaluations in Ohio. In April, 1955, the State Board of Tax Appeals in Akron ruled that the advent of Negro residents into a "white neighborhood" does not necessarily reduce property values. And a vivid illustration of this ruling was shown by a Columbus builder of houses selling at $10,-000 with no down payment and 40-year mortgages. As a result of an open-occupancy provision, these homes were sold to both white and colored and no racial incidents developed. Real estate values actually went up in consequence of the rehabilitation of the neighborhood.

VOTING

Little if any discrimination has been found to exist in Ohio voting practices.

EDUCATION

Ohio schools on all levels appear to be integrated and only a few instances of discriminatory patterns have been reported. In 1956, the Ohio Attorney General ruled that the State Board of Education is empowered to withhold funds from school districts or boards permitting segregation. Of course, the problem is aggravated by the existence of Negro housing segregation. Often the requirement of attendance at schools nearest to the home practically dictates attendance at segregated schools.

EMPLOYMENT

Definite discrimination in Ohio employment was the impetus for the establishment of the Ohio Civil Rights Commission. The commission is entrusted with the administration of the Ohio FEPC law which prohibits discrimination on the grounds of race, color, religion, ancestry or national origin by employers, labor organizations and employment agencies. Private employers of four or more are covered by the law.

Many Ohio Negroes have been severely handicapped in their professional advancement as a result of the refusal of various craft labor unions to admit Negro applicants into their apprenticeship training programs. This debarment means virtual exclusion of all Negroes from promotion to skilled positions. Many unions have recently adopted a more liberal policy in this respect. Thus, for example, in April of 1957, AFL–CIO President George Meany ordered the Cleveland local of the International Brotherhood of Electrical Workers to end discrimination against Negro applicants or face loss of its charter. Similarly, in Cleveland, in January, 1960, the Brotherhood of Railroad Trainmen dropped racial bars to union membership.

HOUSING

Most Ohio Negroes live in inadequate, unsafe and unsanitary buildings. They occupy the older parts of the cities and rent obsolete and inferior apartments at high rates. The complete absence of appropriate state or local legislation has thwarted any serious efforts to remedy this situation. Community relations boards, mayors' committees and similar groups have sought to ease the consequences ensuing from the residential patterns. Grass-roots initiative has been instrumental in the improvement of the situation in a number of instances. In July, 1959, over 200 families in Shaker Heights, Cleveland, organized to preserve the integrated neighborhood and "create a workable plan for democratic living among Negro and white families in the suburb."

PUBLIC ACCOMMODATIONS

Hotels, motels, golf courses, tennis courts, public beaches and swimming pools still practice open discrimination against Negroes and, to a lesser extent, Jews in certain areas of Ohio. The Coney Island amusement park in Cincinnati was closed to Negroes until May, 1961, when three attempts to gain admission to this segregated facility by 24 members of CORE and the NAACP led to desegregation.

In June of 1955 the Ohio Turnpike Commission announced it would not publicize any establishment along the turnpike practicing discrimination. Following an appeal by the Ohio Civil Rights Commission, Governor DiSalle urged passage of appropriate legislation to strengthen the prohibition against discrimination in places of public accommodation and to vest jurisdiction in the Civil Rights Commission.

INTERRACIAL MARRIAGE

Ohio has no law prohibiting interracial marriage.

OKLAHOMA

"While Oklahoma has made real progress in the area of integration in its public school system at all levels, there are still many problems and it is the feeling of this committee that Oklahoma may be getting too much favorable publicity and some of it no doubt paints the picture brighter than it really is."

REPORT OF THE OKLAHOMA ADVISORY COMMITTEE
TO THE U.S. COMMISSION ON CIVIL RIGHTS

The Negro population is about 8% of the total population. In 15 counties there are no Negro children and in 32 counties the non-white population constitutes less than 5% of the whole. In all Oklahoma counties except five some steps toward school desegregation had been taken by 1959. This fairly impressive record is, however, marred by the fact that in the process of integration many Negro teachers have lost their positions. While only 10 or 20 Negro teachers are currently employed in the state's mixed schools, 344 have lost their jobs. And the opinion has been stated that most of the latter are as well qualified as their white colleagues.

VOTING

Oklahoma has had a long history of ingenious attempts to deny Negroes their right to exercise the vote. For many years the famous "grandfather clause," a device similar to others which had been adopted earlier by southern states, was sufficient insurance. Under this clause a literacy test based on the ability to read and write any section of the Oklahoma constitution was mandatory for Negro applicants. The law generously provided a loophole for illiterate whites by exempting all citizens whose ancestors were qualified to vote as of January 1, 1866. This was, of course, a date when no Negro in the state would have been qualified to vote.

This Oklahoma law was struck down by the U.S. Supreme Court

in 1915 as a violation of the 15th Amendment. Negroes and other groups meet with little appreciable discrimination in voting registration in Oklahoma today.

EDUCATION

A survey of all Oklahoma school districts has revealed that desegregation is in effect in 188 of the 250 biracial districts. Of the state's estimated 40,000 Negro students, 30,000 were considered to be in "integrated situations." An earlier, more detailed appraisal showed that in 1958 there were 168 integrated elementary schools, 101 integrated junior high schools, and 190 integrated high schools. Oklahoma Christian College will admit Negroes for the first time in 1961.

EMPLOYMENT

Oklahoma has not taken any steps to enact an FEPC law. There is acknowledgment of considerable discrimination in the hiring and employment of Negroes and Indians. Although some liberality has been observed in the big cities, there is a general reluctance to modify traditional discriminatory practices.

Oklahoma Negroes are employed only in unskilled jobs and those who are semi-skilled or trained craftsmen find it almost impossible to obtain positions commensurate with their training and experience. The Tulsa Urban League, which has been engaged in quiet but firm attempts to improve the situation, believes that the lack of suitable antidiscrimination legislation makes improvement difficult.

HOUSING

Most of Oklahoma's Negro population is located in the southeastern section along the Texas border. This is known as the "Little Dixie" area and it maintains a segregated housing pattern consistent with its southern locality. No estimate has been made of the degree of substandard occupancy by Negroes but it is tacitly agreed to be proportionally high. The usual reasons are present: unavailability of FHA financing, unwillingness of local realtors to rent or sell to Negroes, and the minority group's low economic purchasing power.

PUBLIC ACCOMMODATIONS

By Oklahoma law segregation is mandatory in many transportation and recreational facilities. Immediately upon becoming a state in 1907 Oklahoma initiated segregation in several aspects of public accommodation. Later, parks, libraries, hotels and restaurants were segregated until, by 1954, the policy of rigid segregation was complete.

INTERRACIAL MARRIAGE

Marriage is prohibited in the state between persons of African descent and persons of other descent.

OREGON

"When we came to the county in 1952, we were assured not once but several times by agents that all of the county was 'such a nice place to live because there are no colored people here.' A back country native told us of 20 acres of good soil he was sure he could buy at a reasonable figure since it was owned by a Negro war veteran in Los Angeles who would never be permitted to live on it. There is no known organized opposition to persons of color, but as soon as one tries to take up residence in the area, he is immediately threatened with violence."

FROM A RESPONSE TO A LETTER SENT BY THE OREGON STATE ADVISORY COMMITTEE TO THE U.S. COMMISSION ON CIVIL RIGHTS TO VARIOUS COMMUNITIES IN OREGON IN 1958

Although Negroes constitute less than one per cent of the total population in Oregon, their housing situation is the most deplorable. The 3,500 Japanese-Americans and the 2,400 Chinese-Americans in the state meet with much less discrimination in the purchase and rental of housing accommodations in large cities than the Negroes.

Mexican-Americans and Indians living off the reservations meet with almost the same amount of discrimination as the Negroes. State and local authorities have recently shown increasing concern with this pattern and have begun to initiate programs which are intended to bring relief to minority groups by the provision of more adequate housing facilities.

VOTING

Available evidence points to the absence of discriminatory practices in Oregon registration and voting. Minority groups are permitted to exercise their voting rights fully and freely.

EDUCATION

Oregon schools are integrated in all grades. There is some inevitable segregation in the all-Negro residential neighborhoods based on the need to attend schools in the vicinity.

EMPLOYMENT

Oregon has enacted an FEPC law which makes discrimination on the grounds of race, color, religion, age or national origin by employers, labor organizations and employment agencies an illegal practice. The right to employment without discrimination is acknowledged to be a civil right. The law is administered by the Oregon Civil Rights Division.

There is evidence of discrimination against Negroes and Mexican-Americans who are often unable to find jobs commensurate with their qualifications or are excluded from training opportunities which are indispensable prerequisites for admission to those unions which monopolize certain trades.

HOUSING

A report issued by the Portland City Club in 1957 stated that 50% of Portland's minority groups occupied substandard housing at that time. No privately built housing was available to them and less than 200 families had moved into publicly-built houses in recent years.

Builders and real estate boards still engage in open discrimination to preserve all-white neighborhoods. Urban renewal programs in Florence, Springfield and Portland have not yet gone beyond the discussion stage.

In the Eugene–Springfield area the housing situation has improved and several Negroes of good financial standing have been able to purchase or rent houses or apartments in formerly all-white areas. The contention that property values decrease with the influx of Negroes into white neighborhoods was disproved by the results of a study made by the Urban League in Portland. It revealed a gain in property values of 27.7% in five tested areas where non-whites had purchased homes; while in five other control-areas where nonwhites had not entered the gain in average price was 28.7%; only 1% difference. To all intents and purposes then, the gain in real estate values was the same in integrated and nonintegrated neighborhoods.

On May 25, 1959, Governor Hatfield signed a law which made Oregon the fourth state of the union to prohibit discrimination in the sale or occupancy of private housing.

PUBLIC ACCOMMODATIONS

Oregon beauty parlors, barber shops and "health studios" have regularly practiced discrimination. Instances of refusal to be accepted as patients have also been reported by Negroes seeking medical or dental care from white doctors or dentists. Certain motels and hotels do not cater to Negro clients. State Senator Lewis recently introduced a bill to amend the existing law against discrimination in places of public accommodation by adding "any place where public goods or services are offered." This amendment would reach, among other places, doctors' and dentists' offices, barber shops and beauty salons.

The Oregon Civil Rights Law provides for civil action for damages not exceeding $500 to a person discriminated against in the use of public accommodations. The law also provides for a criminal penalty of a $1,000 fine and one year in jail for willful violation of a cease-and-desist order of the Commission of Labor which administers civil rights laws in the state.

INTERRACIAL MARRIAGE

A state law banning interracial marriage was repealed in 1951 and Oregon law no longer prohibits marriages between white and members of other racial groups.

PENNSYLVANIA

"When 400 ministers in one city advise their congregations not to buy something, a lot of whatever that something may be goes unbought and the company that makes it is quickly aware of the fact. In March 1961, 400 Philadelphia Negro ministers inaugurated their Selective Patronage Program. Their purpose is simple and forthright: to persuade one company after another in Philadelphia to employ more Negroes in prestige jobs. A delegation of four or five ministers calls on the company and requests it to hire a certain number of Negro workers in such jobs as truck drivers or office clerks. The company is given a deadline to comply with this request and, in case of failure to comply, a boycott is called from 400 pulpits. After such boycotts had greatly reduced the sales of the Pepsi-Cola, the Gulf Oil and the Tasty Baking Companies, they all hired the requested number of Negroes and the boycotts were then called off."

HANNAH LEE, "THE NOT-BUYING POWER OF PHILADELPHIA'S NEGROES,"
The Reporter, MAY 11, 1961

Although Pennsylvania has had an FEPC for a number of years, more actual progress in the improvement of employment opportunities for Negroes has been attained in the last year when the Negro community initiated its formidably successful boycott. Already the Bond Bread, Freihofer Bread, Coca-Cola, 7-Up, Esso, Cities Service, Atlantic and Mobile corporations have found the ministers' pressure irresistible and have hired Negro employees. All of the personnel departments of the companies concerned have been quoted as being pleased with the calibre of the new employees.

VOTING

A thorough analysis of voting laws, registration procedures and actual registration data has indicated that there is no legally sanctioned or administratively imposed discrimination in regard to the voting rights of any minority group in Pennsylvania.

EDUCATION

No deliberate discriminatory practices have been found to exist in any of the public school districts of Pennsylvania. State-controlled and state-assisted institutions of higher learning do not exercise any discrimination with regard to race, creed or color in their admission policies.

Certain state-aided universities in Pennsylvania have been accused of discriminating against Jewish applicants in admission to their medical schools. Since no inquiries are made by these medical schools concerning the religion or race of prospective candidates, it is difficult to legally substantiate these claims.

The newly created Pennsylvania Human Relations Commission has been given jurisdiction over discrimination on all levels of the educational system from kindergarten to postgraduate studies.

EMPLOYMENT

A large incidence of discrimination is prevalent in all branches of industry in the state. Some 89% of 1,200 firms employing 900,000 employees in 44 communities containing 80% of Pennsylvania's total population were found to discriminate in some way against minority groups in employment in 1954. There has not been any dramatic reversal in sentiment since then except in the Philadelphia instance. Besides the improvements achieved through the Selective Patronage Program of the 400 Negro ministers in Philadelphia, many other Pennsylvania communities have recognized the reality of discrimination in employment by the establishment of community councils to work on the problem. In February, 1961, the name of the existing FEPC was changed to the Pennsylvania

Human Relations Commission with a subsequent increase in the scope of its powers.

HOUSING

Housing discrimination in Pennsylvania is omnipresent and directed not only against Negroes but also against Jews, Italians, Puerto Ricans and other ethnic groups. Segregation is practiced in private housing as well as in low-rent housing projects built with federal subsidies. In this state, 80% of the Negroes in the big cities dwell in segregated neighborhoods. Negroes almost invariably live in old structures: 98% of the Negroes in Philadelphia inhabit housing built before 1930 and many of these were erected before 1900. Jews have great difficulty renting or purchasing in the suburbs of large cities such as Philadelphia's Main Line or Pittsburgh's South Hills. Almost all real estate dealers refuse to place Negro families in all-white sections. Out of 200,000 dwelling units built in Philadelphia between 1947 and 1953, less than 1% was available to Negroes. Urban renewal projects displace many Negroes who then cannot find housing except in ghetto neighborhoods which then become even more overcrowded than before through this acceleration of the deterioration.

Some voluntary attempts to break the pattern of complete segregation in Pennsylvania have proved fruitful. A good example is the East Millsboro development which integrated Negro miners' families into a white neighborhood. Another is the Concord Park development in suburban Philadelphia. Governor Lawrence signed an antidiscriminatory housing law which became effective on September 1, 1961.

PUBLIC ACCOMMODATIONS

Pennsylvania laws stemming from 1917 and incorporated into the Penal Code of 1939, declare that all persons in the Commonwealth shall be entitled to full and equal accommodations and privileges. Nevertheless, numerous instances of discrimination in hotels, motels and resort facilities are constantly brought to the attention of the Pennsylvania Human Relations Commission. Racial discrimination in the hotels of downtown Philadelphia and Pittsburgh has been largely eliminated. Compliance with the Hotel and Motel Association's official antidiscriminatory stand, however, has not been complete.

Many state-supported hospitals in Pennsylvania still do not afford equal opportunities to Negro physicians who are thereby prevented from following their patients' treatment in the hospital.

INTERRACIAL MARRIAGE

Pennsylvania has no law banning interracial marriage.

RHODE ISLAND

"There is such little representation of minority group peoples in banks, insurance companies and public utilities that it must be the aim of the Commission to seek improvement."

FROM THE ANNUAL REPORT OF THE
RHODE ISLAND FAIR EMPLOYMENT COMMISSION

Insurance, financial, as well as public utility institutions in Rhode Island, have heretofore excluded Jews from employment in managerial and executive positions although it is admitted many qualified Jewish candidates have applied. These enterprises also refrain from hiring qualified Negroes and, to a lesser extent, qualified Jews, for clerical and other white-collar jobs.

The existence of stringent FEPC laws in Rhode Island has not assured the elimination of discrimination in the state. But this must be viewed in relation to Rhode Island's achievement in combating discrimination, which is considerable. An insurance executive has remarked: "There are subtle ways of staying inside the law such as hiring a token force of minority workers." A Rhode Island bank president when asked by a Community Relations Committee to abandon the prevailing pattern of segregation in his bank by hiring several Jews and Negroes, stated: "We have always given a fair chance to all applicants, no matter whether they were Jews, Negroes, or Hottentots." His bank numbered one Negro elevator operator and one Jewish file clerk among its employees at the time.

VOTING

Members of minority groups appear to enjoy fully equal voting rights in Rhode Island and there are few complaints concerning the abridgment of the right to register and vote on the state's record.

EDUCATION

Rhode Island has a statutory prohibition against discrimination or segregation in public education. Public education on all levels is integrated and members of minority groups are not discriminated against. The number of Negro teachers is, however, disproportionally small. This is said to be due to the fact that until recently relatively few Negroes possessed the qualifications required by the Rhode Island Board of Education.

The Rhode Island College of Education has increased its enrollment of Negroes during the last few years and there are some prospects for the employment of a larger number of Negro teachers in the future. Negro teachers have been accepted by pupils, fellow-teachers and parents. In both the Rhode Island College of Education and the University of Rhode Island, the two public institutions of higher learning in the state, there are no restrictions as to race, color, national origin or creed. On both campuses Negroes are fully accepted.

EMPLOYMENT

As previously indicated, discrimination in employment in Rhode Island is widespread. In 1949, the state established an independent Commission Against Discrimination which administers an FEPC law covering employers of four or more, labor organizations and employment agencies. Discrimination on the grounds of race, color, religion or national origin is prohibited. Of the complaints received by the commission, 88% charged discrimination on account of race or color. Although Rhode Island has enacted adequate legislation little voluntary antidiscriminatory activity has emerged on the community level. The lack of this community involvement in reducing employment discrimination has resulted in the high incidence of such discrimination described above.

HOUSING

Some 90% of Rhode Island's Negroes live in substandard housing. None of the state's housing is available on an open-occupancy basis. Negroes who have attained some business or professional eminence find it very difficult to rent appropriate living quarters. The Rhode Island Subcommittee on Housing carried out a study which established that Providence housing projects rented solely by income criteria. Approximately 15% of the units in these projects are now occupied by nonwhites. No precipitate departures followed the admission of the Negro families and integration was accomplished without hostile incidents.

On February 20, 1961, Governor John A. Notte appointed a citizens committee to consider and recommend legislation designed to eliminate discrimination in state housing.

PUBLIC ACCOMMODATIONS

Discrimination and segregation are prohibited in public accommodations in Rhode Island. Sufficient evidence is on record to indicate that the state has not, however, succeeded in completely eliminating such practices.

INTERRACIAL MARRIAGE

Rhode Island has no law prohibiting marriage between whites and Negroes or other races.

SOUTH CAROLINA

"Eight Friendship Junior College students and I served 30 days on the York County road gang for the 'crime' of sitting-in at McCrory's lunch counter in Rock Hill, South Carolina. While hundreds of students have been jailed since the start of the sit-in movement, we were the first to be committed to a road gang, which is the present-day version of the dreaded southern chain gang.

"We could have paid $100 fines, or we could have posted $200 bail each and gone out pending appeal. Instead, we chose to be jailed-in. All nine of us felt that this would strengthen the impact of our protest. Furthermore, instead of the city being $900 richer for the injustice it had committed, it would have to pay the expense of boarding us for 30 days."

THOMAS GAITHER, *Jailed-In*, THE LEAGUE FOR INDUSTRIAL DEMOCRACY

Despite the tenacity of young college students such as Thomas Gaither—a CORE field secretary—sit-ins in South Carolina have not yet integrated a single lunch-counter. On March 15, 1960, over 350 Negroes who had participated in a mass demonstration against lunch-counter segregation were arrested and, when they overflowed the Orangeburg jail, were herded into an open-air stockade. It was on this occasion that Governor Hollings asserted that such demonstrations would not be tolerated, adding: "They think they can violate any law, especially if they have a Bible in their hands."

VOTING

Although Negroes constituted 33.9% of the total voting-age population in South Carolina in 1950, they represented only 10.8% of all registered voters. While 63% of all eligible whites were registered voters, only 15% of all eligible Negroes had been entered onto the registration books. In 1950 the poll tax was abolished in South Carolina as a prerequisite for voting. It also appears certain that only a fraction of those Negroes who have been successful in registering are actually able to vote as a consequence of various discriminatory obstructions employed against them at the time of elections.

EDUCATION

There had been, as of 1961, no desegregation in South Carolina schools since the Supreme Court decision. The state is one of the five that framed so-called interposition resolutions calling the 1954 ruling an illegal encroachment upon the reserved powers of the states and advocating all-out resistance to its implementation. It is one of the three states that still had no desegregation as of 1961.

In preparation for the eventual closing of public schools in the event of federal insistence upon carrying out desegregation, the South Carolina legislature repealed the compulsory school attendance law in 1954. A year later a law was adopted providing for a stoppage of state appropriations and state aid for any school from or to which any pupil was transferred by court order. It was further provided that this stoppage should cease only when the pupil involved returned to the school to which he had been assigned prior to the court order.

Before 1895, South Carolina had a law prohibiting segregation in public schools. After that year the policy of strict racial separation in public schools has been strictly followed. Rather than face integration, South Carolina sought for several years to preserve racial segregation by the difficult and expensive "separate but equal" doctrine. Whenever a court determined a deprivation of educational opportunities for Negroes, the state would establish the requested graduate or professional school in one of the state colleges for Negroes.

In 1956, South Carolina incorporated a provision into the general appropriations bill making segregation an essential for the receipt of state funds and declaring that if any state college was closed on that ground the state would also close the South Carolina

State College for Negroes. Another provision of the same law prohibited the employment of any member of the NAACP by the
state. It directed the board of trustees of all state colleges to de-
mand an affidavit of nonmembership from each teacher or other
employee. When 90% of the faculty at South Carolina State College for Negroes refused to disavow the NAACP and an almost
100% student strike was called to protest the state's segregation
policies, only the direct intervention of the governor ended the
crisis. The president of the student council and 15 other students
were expelled; the contracts of three faculty members were not
renewed and several other teachers voluntarily left the college.

In 1957, South Carolina established a State Sovereignty Commission in order to preserve total segregation in the state's system of
higher education. Clemson College renounced a $350,000 federal
grant from the Atomic Energy Commission in the same year and
returned $99,000 already received rather than comply with the
antidiscriminatory stipulations embodied in the grant.

On the high school level, South Carolina spent about 500%
more for each white than for each Negro citizen in 1957–58.

EMPLOYMENT

There is considerable discrimination against Negroes in South Carolina employment. They are generally afforded no opportunity to
obtain jobs commensurate with their qualifications and they are
denied admission to training programs in the various crafts. They
fail to receive promotions beyond certain well-defined categories
and the state's unions have not yet changed their generally acqui-
escent attitude toward segregation. In July of 1961, the NAACP
Labor Secretary Herbert Hill drew national attention to the discriminatory labor practices at the Charleston Naval Yard. As a result
of the President's Committee on Government Contracts review of
the charges the employment practices have changed at the yard.

HOUSING

South Carolina's Negroes live in segregated areas of the big cities
and dilapidated shanty-towns in the country. Housing conditions

are universally poor, unsanitary and substandard in the city or the country. No action has been taken by state authorities to alleviate the situation. Negroes who have been able to acquire the necessary financial resources for the purchase of decent housing are not permitted to buy or rent in the all-white sections of South Carolina.

PUBLIC ACCOMMODATIONS

South Carolina laws require absolute segregation of the races in all types of public accommodations including transportation. Hotels, restaurants, lunch counters, swimming pools, barber shops, bowling alleys, waiting rooms, railroads, bus companies and public parks including state parks are all operated on a racially segregated basis. In July, 1961, a suit to integrate South Carolina's twenty-three state-supported parks and recreation areas was filed in the U.S. District Court in Charleston by eleven Negroes, including the president of the state NAACP. Five of these 23 parks are reserved for Negroes, the others are for whites only. The plaintiffs contend that a South Carolina law requiring segregation in state parks is unconstitutional in so far as it denies the equal protection and due process guaranteed by the 14th Amendment.

As mentioned earlier, sit-ins at Rock Hills, Orangeburg and other South Carolina cities have not yet led to the desegregation of lunch counters.

INTERRACIAL MARRIAGE

South Carolina laws prohibit marriage between white and Negro or Indian.

SOUTH DAKOTA

"Members of Local 7 of the United Packing House Workers of America have voted not to take vacations in the Black Hills area of South Dakota because of alleged racial discrimination there. The local adopted the resolution, a union official said, because a Negro doctor was refused restaurant service in Rapid City."

ASSOCIATED PRESS, JUNE 22, 1961

Although Indians are the only minority group of substantial number (about 5% of the population) living in South Dakota, the state's civil rights practice is important because of the increasing attraction of the Black Hills, Mount Rushmore country to tourists of all races.

The Indian peoples of South Dakota live in two different patterns: on-reservation and off-reservation. Every facet of life is different in the two situations.

There are also a number of Hutterite colonies in the state but as it is an important part of the beliefs of this sect to remain completely aloof from the world around them, an examination of their civil rights is probably not pertinent.

VOTING

An old South Dakota law, that was not repealed until 1939, held that Indians could not vote in the state. However, it had long been recognized that this statute was an archaic throwback to the Indian uprisings of the previous century, and Indians were actually permitted to vote in South Dakota long before its repeal. The Hutterites do not vote out of religious conviction.

EDUCATION

Indian education in South Dakota is handled by two principal agencies. For Indians on the reservation, education is received from the federally operated Indian schools. Those Indians who live off the reservation attend South Dakota public schools.

There is no discrimination in South Dakota education. Any Indian child can enroll in a public school by satisfying the residence requirement. The federal boarding and day schools have physical plants and teaching staffs generally equivalent to the public schools.

All colleges and universities in South Dakota accept all students without regard to race.

EMPLOYMENT

The state has no law barring discrimination in private employment. Indians, the major minority group in South Dakota, have little opportunity for skilled or well-paying employment.

HOUSING

Reservation Indians live in unqualifiedly squalid housing.

Off the reservation Indians also occupy substandard housing. Segregation is the almost universal pattern. South Dakota landlords have been known to not rent to Indians because of alleged destructive tendencies on the part of the race.

PUBLIC ACCOMMODATIONS

South Dakota has no law prohibiting or requiring discrimination or segregation by private enterprises. A development that has recently come to attention in the state is the treatment accorded to minority group tourists. South Dakota is caught between its expressed desire to encourage travel to its famous scenic attractions and the desire of many Negroes to come into the state for just that purpose. Several dormant discriminatory traditions have been revealed in the welcome the state has not extended to Negro visitors.

INTERRACIAL MARRIAGE

A former law prohibiting marriage between Caucasian and African, Korean, Malayan or Mongolian has been repealed.

TENNESSEE

"It is true that laws alone cannot change the hearts of man. Laws cannot persuade our white brothers to love us. But laws have finally dissuaded them from lynching us. Only when American Negroes attain their full constitutional rights will they be on a basis of political equality from which a meaningful integration into American life can be realized. Of all the rights that we Negroes are denied, the most basic and most essential is the right to vote."

REV. MARTIN LUTHER KING; A SPEECH AT SYRACUSE UNIVERSITY

A new city has arisen in western Tennessee during the past year and it has become a symbol of the most celebrated and unyielding denial of Negro voting rights in the South. It is a "tent city" and is all the home there is to hundreds of Negroes in Haywood and Fayette counties who have been dispossessed and forced from their land because they attempted to register to vote. (See "Voting," below.)

The inhabitants of the dreary, makeshift "tent city" live under temporary shelter provided by the NAACP, CORE, the American Friends Service Committee, the UAW, and countless smaller organizations. They survive on food and medicines trucked in by these same agencies and many northern community committees. The Red Cross has ruled they are ineligible for disaster relief. Since the advent of the new national administration in 1961, they have been receiving supplies from the surpluses of the U.S. Department of Agriculture.

VOTING

In 1956 some 90,000 or 28% of the Negroes in Tennessee were registered to vote. In all counties of the state except three, Negroes were and are freely permitted to register and to vote and have met with little discrimination. In the three counties, all in western Tennessee—Haywood, Fayette and Hardman—actual physical intimidation has prevented anything but token registration. Haywood and Fayette counties have been the most intractable.

Haywood County has a Negro population majority of 61%, but of its 7,921 voting-age Negroes, none was registered until May, 1960. In Fayette County with a Negro majority of 70% only 58 out of 8,990 voting-age Negroes were registered in 1959; voting records showed that of these 58 registrants, one had voted in 1958, 12 in 1953, and three in 1952.

Negroes have not been permitted to register and vote in Haywood County for approximately 50 years. Although they own more land and pay more taxes than the white community, their rights are systematically curtailed. Negroes in the county are forced to observe a strict curfew, they are not permitted to dance or drink beer and are not allowed in the vicinity of the courthouse unless on business.

When a Negro registered to vote in Fayette County, the sheriff was immediately informed. He, in turn, informed the Negro's landlord and employer. The registrant was promptly fired from his job and removed from his home by credit foreclosure. This was particularly easy to accomplish as the majority of the Negroes were sharecroppers.

The employment of economic pressure against Negroes registering was similar in both counties. Arrest and severe fines on minor charges was followed by the withholding of wages, elimination of credit and orders to quit the community.

Early in 1959, a Negro former schoolteacher, with a Master's Degree, filed a complaint with the Tennessee State Advisory Committee to the U.S. Commission on Civil Rights charging that he had met with constant subterfuge and refusal in his attempts to register to vote in Haywood. Since then the conflict between the white and Negro communities in both counties has raged incessantly. The whites appear to be determined to resist Negro registration to the last, despite state and national dismay, reasoning that once they admit the Negro majorities to the franchise the entire natures of the two counties will change. The Negroes have lost so much in economic reprisal, there is little left to lose. The institution of a suit against Haywood County by the U.S. Department of Justice in September, 1960, and the decision of the government to allow surplus agricultural stocks to be distributed to the "tent-city" the Negroes were driven into, has led them to reason that they will prevail in the long run.

EDUCATION

Tennessee was one of the nine southern states to declare its open defiance of the 1954 Supreme Court decision, labeling it an encroachment upon the reserved powers of the states and vowing to resist it with every means. There are now a total of 79 Negro children enrolled in nonsegregated public schools in the state. Catholic parochial schools were opened to Negroes in 1954.

In January, 1956, Clinton High School in Anderson County (3.1% Negro population) was ordered by a Federal District Court to begin desegregation not later than the next fall. Fifteen Negroes enrolled and of these, 12 appeared on opening day. John Kasper, Executive Secretary of the Seaboard's White Citizens' Council, also arrived at the school that day.

Kasper, a professional agitator, soon managed to arouse a town mob to action. Finally, after threatening violence at a mass meeting of more than 1,200 white citizens, Kasper was served with a warrant, temporarily impeding him from resisting desegregation. He was later found guilty of contempt and sentenced to imprisonment for one year on August 31, 1956. Disorders at the school and personal attacks upon the Negro students followed, but by September 15, the high school was operating on a normal basis.

On February 14, 1957, a suitcase full of dynamite exploded in the heart of the Negro section of Clinton, injuring two persons. But the first year of desegregation in Clinton High School ended quietly on May 17 with the graduation of the school's first Negro. On October 5, 1957, a blast of dynamite destroyed a substantial part of

Clinton High and the school had to resort to temporary quarters in
Oak Ridge, 12 miles away. The governor promised his aid and
school board officials applied to the federal government for help
in rebuilding the school.

Nashville initiated a gradual desegregation program in September, 1957. It began with the first grade and will proceed to desegregate one additional grade per year. When 19 Negro first-graders
enrolled, immediate violence erupted including a dynamite blast
that ripped off the roof of the desegregated school. But with decisive action by the mayor and the police department, order was
restored and in the following year 34 Negro first- and second-grad-
ers entered formerly all-white schools in Nashville without incident.

Knoxville is committed to start desegregation in accordance with
an order issued by the Federal District Court in that city. Altogether,
four districts will initiate voluntary integration programs this fall.

EMPLOYMENT

There is extensive employment discrimination in Tennessee on the
basis of race and color in both public and private places of work.
There is no FEPC.

HOUSING

Negroes inhabit substandard homes in completely segregated sections of the bigger cities of Tennessee and are unable to secure adequate living quarters throughout the state. No remedial plans have
been made.

PUBLIC ACCOMMODATIONS

Tennessee is at once a state where until recently complete segregation in the access to all public facilities prevailed, and the home
of many of the most notable and effective young Negro leaders who
have led the assault on these practices throughout the South. The
Reverend James Lawson and Diane Nash, both of the Nashville
Students' Movement, particularly have been successful in "sit-ins"
and "freedom-rides."

INTERRACIAL MARRIAGE

Tennessee law prohibits marriage between white and Negro.

TEXAS

"We thought this should be an adult experience before it is a child experience. If adults couldn't handle it well, we couldn't expect the children to do so."

> STATEMENT BY DALLAS BUSINESS LEADER ABOUT
> VOLUNTARY DESEGREGATION OF DALLAS RES-
> TAURANTS AND CAFETERIAS ON JULY 26, 1961

"Well, you know I protested integration at Tech. First, because it goes against the laws of the sovereign state of Texas. Right there in its charter it says the college will be for white youth only. Second, it goes against the Bible. I've been a Bible teacher for a long time, and the Bible decrees separation in many places. I want to help save the human race from corruption and the Bible tells it time and time again. Third, mixing simply does not work. . . ."

> INTERVIEW WITH TEXAS LADY IN BEAUMONT, TEXAS: *College Desegregation Without Popular Support* BY WARREN BREED,
> ANTI-DEFAMATION LEAGUE

These two conflicting statements and the two incidents they were about represent the divided viewpoints with which Texas has fought and approached the desegregation of many areas of state life in the past few years. The first quotation expresses the voluntary response made by Dallas community leaders to the imminent desegregation of the city's schools in the first grade this year. The second is an earlier comment on a college desegregation.

Texas is split several ways in its attitudes toward desegregation; east Texas versus west Texas, urban versus rural and north versus south. Furthermore, it discriminates in two different ways against two different groups, the Negro and the Mexican-American.

VOTING

Texas has made substantial progress in the elimination of discrimination in voting requirements. Local poll tax levies are still enforced in certain communities. Movements to abolish them have been initiated in many places and there is a definite trend toward the removal of all discriminatory voting practices.

EDUCATION

Gradual desegregation of Texas public schools began in 1954. By the end of 1956, 122 independent school districts in 65 counties were in the process of desegregation. The result of this effort was the enrollment of 3,600 of the state's Negro students (less than 1½% of the total) in mixed schools. The same date found 35 Texas public and private colleges that had taken steps toward integration. In many of these instances it was only token desegregation that was undertaken and that because of prolonged litigation. In January, 1959, North Texas State led in Negro enrollment with 203 among its 6,500 student body. The University of Texas had an estimated 65 Negroes out of 16,000 total registration. The formerly all-Negro St. Philip's Junior College had 635 Negroes and approximately 300 whites.

Desegregation in Texas was brought to a complete standstill in 1956 as a result of various laws passed by the state legislature. Practically no attempt to desegregate existing facilities has yet been made in eastern Texas where the greatest concentration of the Negro population resides. Besides Dallas–Galveston, Lockney and Judson planned to desegregate in the fall of 1961.

EMPLOYMENT

Discrimination in employment is extremely widespread in Texas and extends even to state government jobs. There has been a partial desegregation of the police forces and the postal services in the larger cities. Negroes and Mexican-Americans are rarely hired for clerical positions and are often limited to unskilled jobs even though they may be qualified for higher ratings. Texas has not enacted an FEPC law; only isolated instances of local action has tended to make any significant breaches in the racial employment barriers.

HOUSING

Negroes, and to a lesser extent Mexican-Americans, live in almost entirely segregated and often substandard housing throughout Texas. All federal housing is segregated. The first attempt to alter this time-honored tradition has been made in the West Dallas Federal Housing Project for low-income groups. Of 3,500 units, 1,500 are occupied by whites, the same number by Negroes and 500 by Mexican-Americans. Texas legislators have recommended no anti-discriminatory housing measures.

PUBLIC ACCOMMODATIONS

Public transportation is generally integrated in Texas with the exception of segregated taxi services in various communities. Hotels, motels and restaurants all discriminate against Negroes, Mexicans, Orientals and Jews in varying degrees. Waiting rooms, rest rooms, swimming pools, golf courses and bowling alleys are nearly totally segregated. Most change in public accommodations practice in Texas has occurred in the larger cities. Besides the example noted above of Dallas restaurants, that city and Houston had earlier desegregated their municipal golf courses and beaches.

Negroes in Harris County had to bring legal action in a Federal District Court to restrain county officials from preventing their race from being served in a restaurant in the county courthouse.

INTERRACIAL MARRIAGE

Texas law forbids marriage between Caucasian (white) and African (Negro).

UTAH

"The birth into any race other than the white race is a result of inferior performance in a pre-earth life. By righteous living, the dark-skinned races may again become white and delightsome."

MORMON DOCTRINE

Civil rights and liberties in Utah are inextricably bound up with the unique history of the state and its principal religion, Mormonism. Perhaps 70% of the population of Utah are adherents of the Church of Jesus Christ of Latter-day Saints (Mormon) and almost every aspect of Utah life reflects Mormon theology and bitter memories of early persecution of the Church.

The population of Utah is 98% white. Significant minorities living in the state are Greek, Indian, Japanese-American, Mexican-American, Negro and Jewish. There are sharp differences in the discriminatory practices followed in Utah toward each of these groups. Jews enjoy almost an unprecedented lack of discrimination while Negroes are the object of unusually severe restrictions for a western community.

VOTING

There is no discrimination in the right of minority groups to register and vote in Utah. Even the Indians of the state, many of whom live on federal reservations, are encouraged to exercise their franchise.

EDUCATION

Mexican-Americans have historically suffered the greatest deprivation of educational opportunity in Utah. It is believed that this discrimination has practically ceased in the last few years except in the case of migratory workers who are constantly traveling, and are unable to enroll their children in any one school in successive terms. Indians receive segregated education in Utah, of course, because they continue to live on government reservations. It is generally acknowledged that this is one of the most important factors impeding Indian assimilation. Other minority groups in the state attend integrated schools except to the extent residential segregation imposes local segregated patterns.

EMPLOYMENT

The only minorities free from employment discrimination in Utah are the Greeks and the Jews. The former were once rigidly limited to manual labor but now have access to almost all employment categories in the state. Citizens of Greek origin, now the largest minority in Utah, include a large proportion of wealthy men.

Jewish citizens are prominent in all the professions, business, political, educational and civic circles in Utah. A significant number of them are among the higher economic and cultural strata.

The Negro, Mexican-American and Japanese-American are limited to the least desirable jobs in Utah. In practice, this is effected by not letting these groups even compete for certain positions.

HOUSING

The Negro is the minority citizen who experiences the most widespread housing discrimination and segregation in Utah. Confined by "gentlemen's-agreements" to substandard homes, Utah Negroes have little or no chance to acquire a decent home.

Mexican-Americans in the cities realize almost the same treatment upon housing application as the Negro. In the country, their situation is, if anything, even worse than that of the Negroes.

PUBLIC ACCOMMODATIONS

Public accommodation is the area where Utah's Mormon heritage is most pervasive in contemporary practice. Indians, the oldest inhabitants of the state (in Utah, they are either Utes or Navajos), have absolutely no access to any public accommodations in Utah except the tavern.

The full extent of the discrimination directed at the Negro in Utah is almost impossible to ascertain. They are not admitted to barber shops, beauty parlors or steam rooms at all and their admission to cafes or hotels is arbitrary and infrequent. The Mormon dogma of excluding the Negro from their universal priesthood does not extend to any other race.

Mexican-Americans and Japanese-Americans are the recipients of far less discrimination in public accommodations. This rather unpredictable situation is rendered even more amazing when it is recalled that the former shares the Negro's exclusion in housing and employment opportunities, and the latter suffered great hostility and inequality during World War II when, as so-called enemy aliens, they were sent to Utah.

Anti-Semitism is only encountered in certain social and fraternal organizations and Greek citizens are now welcomed in every phase of Utah life.

INTERRACIAL MARRIAGE

Perhaps the most offensive restriction to the Japanese-American community in Utah is the ancient state law forbidding marriage between an Oriental and Caucasian.

VERMONT

"An interesting contrast is provided by our findings in New York and Vermont which border on one another. In New York State, where a Public Accommodation Law is vigorously enforced, we found that only eight percent of the examined hotels are discriminatory. In Vermont, which has no law against discrimination by hotels, 45% discriminate."

ALBERT WEISS, *Resorts,* A NATIONAL SURVEY PUBLISHED BY THE
ANTI-DEFAMATION LEAGUE

Jewish and Negro tourists eager to see the scenically beautiful state of Vermont have frequently been refused accommodations in certain hotels or motels which preferred to cater to a "restricted clientele." In 1957, the Vermont legislature enacted a statute prohibiting discrimination in places of public resort. Since then the situation appears to have materially improved. This statute was preceded by a ruling of the Vermont Attorney General in May, 1956, to the effect that resorts practicing racial discrimination may not be listed in official state tourist publications.

VOTING

Vermont has no discrimination in voting on the basis of color, race or creed. It requires, however, a poll tax to be paid prior to exercising the franchise by all those eligible for voting in local and state elections. As members of the minority groups, especially the Negroes, frequently fail to qualify on account of their inability to pay the tax, this requirement indirectly contributes to the deprivation of their voting rights. That Vermont is not inclined to abandon this discriminatory practice was shown by the defeat of a bill to repeal local poll taxes in the legislature in 1959.

EDUCATION

There is no evidence of discrimination in Vermont public education on account of race. Negroes are able to find employment as teachers if they possess the required qualifications. In the college town of Middlebury, Negroes have been employed as teachers for some time. Several instances of discrimination on religious grounds have been detected in Vermont, but community pressure resulted in the retention of the teachers in question.

EMPLOYMENT

Vermont has not yet taken any steps to enact an FEPC law. Little research has been conducted in the area of employment discrimination in the state although there is some evidence that Negroes find the securing of jobs above the unskilled level very difficult.

HOUSING

In all regions of Vermont with a substantial concentration of Negroes, housing discrimination is prevalent. These areas include the vicinities of the principal military installations in the state, the counties of Chittenden and Franklin, and the cities of St. Albans, Winooski and Burlington.

Housing discrimination in Vermont was found to extend even to FHA-financed properties. In one verified instance a builder who intended to construct a racially mixed development was warned to abandon the plan by his bank or forfeit his future credit rating.

Under the auspices of Vermont churches, a voluntary citizens' effort in and about the city of Burlington has initiated action to remedy the housing situation by instituting a register which landlords and others can use who make their properties available to Negroes. The lack of appropriate state legislation to eliminate discrimination in the sale or rental of houses and apartments is a serious handicap to these citizen efforts.

PUBLIC ACCOMMODATIONS

In general, Vermont does not have a serious problem of public accommodation discrimination toward any of its own citizens primarily because the nonwhite population of the state is less than 1% of the whole. On the other hand, Vermont derives a large annual income from the flourishing tourist trade and therefore is greatly concerned with the problem of eliminating discrimination in the treatment of minority-group tourists.

INTERRACIAL MARRIAGE

Vermont has no law banning interracial marriage.

VIRGINIA

"The big concern on the part of counsel for the plaintiffs is that the Federal Court will not duck or hide. Recently it has been the trend of federal courts to refer cases of this nature to the state courts. This trend is like telling one to go to the guy who just punched you in the mouth to be protected."

LEONARD W. HOLT, COUNSEL FOR THE PLAINTIFFS
IN A SUIT AGAINST THE CITY OF HOPEWELL, VA.

The "trend of federal courts to refer cases of this nature (i.e., civil rights) to state courts" has been noted frequently in recent Virginia civil rights developments. Undoubtedly the most famous and most basic instance is in that of the Prince Edward County school closing.

In September of 1959, some 1,750 Negro students and 1,500 whites were locked out of the twenty public schools of Prince Edward County. Faced by a federal court desegregation order, the county board of supervisors had voted the previous June to abandon public education rather than consider even token compliance.

Most white students have since been attending privates classes organized by the Prince Edward School Foundation and financed by state and county grants to parents. Only five Negroes have accepted the grants and enrolled in private institutions elsewhere. With the help of the Friends Service Committee, about 300 transferred to public schools outside the county.

NAACP lawyers filed suit to force the reopening of the Prince Edward schools. Maintaining that the tuition grants were, at least in part, derived from public funds, the NAACP contended that this private school system based on "freedom of choice" was nothing but a device to circumvent the United States Court of Appeals order directing the county to admit qualified Negroes to its schools.

In September, 1961 the U.S. Supreme Court ruled Prince Edward tuition grants were indeed circumventory.

VOTING

Virginia is one of the five southern states which have not yet taken any steps to abolish the payment of a poll tax as a prerequisite to voting. In order to be eligible to vote in the state a person must present proof that he has paid the annual poll tax at the rate of $1.50 for at least three consecutive years preceding the six months before the general election. This, of course, results in the actual disfranchisement of a large number of poor but qualified Negro voters. Nonwhites, constituting 21.1% of the total voting-age population of Virginia, were only 9.8% of the state's registered voters in 1958.

EDUCATION

Virginia's school closing laws were invoked first in September, 1958, to withdraw nine public schools from local authority and operation. An estimated 12,729 pupils were affected by these closings and 3,015 were presumed to have remained without any instruction in any school. In all, 17 school districts will have desegregated by this fall.

Only Virginia's Catholic schools began to desegregate in 1954 with the placement of Negro pupils in ten schools. From the very word of the Supreme Court decision, strong segregationist forces under the leadership of Senator Byrd's political machine began "massive resistance" to desegregation. This policy was carried out, primarily, by means of prolonged litigation in state courts. After the state laws, under which the governor's power was invoked to achieve the closing of the public schools, were held to violate both the federal and state constitutions, three Virginia communities were ordered to desegregate in February, 1959. The net result of this token effort was an enrollment of 17 Negroes among 7,200 white students in Norfolk, of four Negroes among 1,075 whites in Arlington, and of nine Negro pupils among 2,300 whites in Alexandria.

Nevertheless, it is significant that in all three communities there was no mob violence or other disturbance of the peace because the local law enforcement agencies made it clear that no defiance would be tolerated.

Prior to 1950, the State of Virginia had recognized its obligation to provide graduate and professional training for its Negro residents by making tuition grants available to qualified applicants. Such training was obtained at a special institution for Negroes in Hampton. However, when Gregory Hayes Swanson, a Negro lawyer from Danville, Virginia, and a graduate of Howard University, applied for admission to the Law School of the University of Virginia as a graduate student in 1950 and was rejected, he obtained an injunction from a Federal District Court to prevent the University of Virginia from denying admission to members of the Negro race as graduate law students. Since that date, most Virginia graduate schools have opened their doors to qualified Negro applicants.

In general, it can be said that only token integration has taken place in the public schools of Virginia. The majority of the state's school boards have preferred this circumvention to the more open defiance of transforming the public schools into a segregated private school system, judging that the Supreme Court will in the last issue declare open defiance unconstitutional. Meanwhile, the plight of those Negro children of Prince Edward County who have been forced to go without any public school education for two years is becoming desperate. Thirty-three teachers of the Virginia Teachers Association gave up part of their vacations last summer to conduct, without pay, a remedial teaching program. One little girl who had never attended school, through no fault of her own, told her family after the first day of summer school: "I'm going to learn to read quicker than anybody you've ever seen."

EMPLOYMENT

Virginia has no FEPC law. Discrimination on the basis of race or color is widespread in state employment and except for those who work in Washington, D.C., job opportunities for Negroes in Virginia above the unskilled level are scarce. There is a small Negro middle class in Virginia made up of bankers, lawyers, physicians, etc., which is primarily occupied in serving the Negro community.

HOUSING

Whereas Negroes constituted over one-third of the total population of Virginia in 1900, they now represent just about one-fifth. This is due to a continuous immigration of whites and emigration of Negroes, principally to and from the North and Midwest. With a population increase of 17.6% from 1950 through 1958, the number of occupied dwelling units in the state increased 228,000 or 27%. This indicates a volume of construction that is more than adequate to the population growth. But it is admitted that Negroes did not receive an adequate share of this new housing; they moved into only about 15% of the new units.

Some effort has been made to relieve the pressure as shown by the fact that the 16 Redevelopment and Housing Authorities in the state now operate or have under construction 14,500 units of which 80% are or will be occupied by nonwhites. Public housing is almost completely on a segregated basis in Virginia.

PUBLIC ACCOMMODATIONS

Desegregation in the use of public facilities has taken place in several of the big towns in Virginia. In some cases this has resulted from court action but essentially it has been the result of Negro sit-in campaigns or other nonviolent agitation on the part of Negro citizens' groups. As early as 1955, a Federal District Court has ruled that racial segregation in state parks was unconstitutional and the same court upheld an injunction to bar discrimination on municipal golf courses in Richmond in 1957. Several of the public transportation systems in Virginia towns have been integrated. The new Golden Triangle Hotel in Norfolk agreed in August, 1961, to provide accommodations for both white and Negro delegates to the AFL–CIO Convention in that city and Edward Dawley, a Norfolk attorney, desegregated a leading Richmond hotel in July of the same year during attendance at the State Republican Party Convention.

A long series of suits, ensuing from a "sit-in" by seven Negroes at a Lynchburg drugstore in 1961 finally concluded with a negotiated settlement. Similarly, a number of other public accommodation settlements were reached in this manner.

INTERRACIAL MARRIAGE

Virginia laws prohibit marriage between white and nonwhite.

WASHINGTON

"Take a man for what he is; not who he is."

FOLKLORE PROVERB OF THE OLD WEST

The State of Washington, keystone of the great Northwest, is significantly advanced in several areas of civil rights. In terms of legislation, the state seems determined to honor the memory of the Code of the Frontier which guaranteed every man the right to earn his place in society. It is indisputable, however, that many of the citizens of the state do not share their government's concern for the welfare of minority groups and considerable discrimination is evident in Washington in housing and employment practices.

In a state as varied as Washington, it is not surprising that conditions and attitudes differ throughout the separate regions. In one sector discrimination in employment is the major problem while in another it is segregated and inadequate housing. It is, therefore, even more necessary than in other states to examine the state of civil rights in Washington on a regional basis.

VOTING

One privilege of citizenship that is administered with equal justice throughout Washington is the right to vote. Very little, if any, discrimination in the right to register and vote has ever existed in the state.

EDUCATION

Discrimination and segregation are prohibited in Washington public schools. Not only is there a policy of nondiscrimination, but there appears to be a conscious effort on the part of school and college authorities to relentlessly bar any discriminatory customs that even vaguely emerge in the educational community. Where there is a concentration of Negroes in a neighborhood because of residential segregation, there is inevitably some school segregation but even this common problem is addressed with uncommon attention by state and local school administrators.

EMPLOYMENT

Discrimination in employment has been prohibited by law for several years in Washington. The Washington State Board Against Discrimination is empowered to receive, initiate, and investigate complaints. Enforcement is vested in the state courts.

Despite this very strong and liberal act, discrimination in Washington employment practice has not been eliminated. Examples vary from locality to locality within the state.

There is not one Negro teacher in Yakima; in Spokane there are seven in addition to one Indian; all popular. A number of Negroes operate gas stations as lessees in Seattle: none work at any of the chain stations. There are two Chinese physicians with white practices in Yakima; most of their fellow Orientals (including Filipinos and Japanese) can only find employment in "stoop" labor that white workers disdain. Negro girls find it extremely difficult to find waitress jobs anywhere in Seattle except in the Bon Marché's New Orleans Room.

There are many aspects of employment discrimination, of course, where minority group opportunity is consistent throughout the state. There is not a single Negro taxi driver in the State of Washington, although the cab companies have been reminded that this is in violation of the fair employment practices law. There is not a single Negro bellhop or porter in a hotel or motel in the state. There is not a single Negro pilot, hostess, ticket-clerk or purser on any of the major airlines using the Tacoma–Seattle airport. There is not a Negro fireman, brakeman, conductor or steward on any of the railroads operating in the state.

HOUSING

In spite of the Washington law which opposes discrimination in the sale of property, decent housing is generally unavailable to minority groups in the state.

An informal survey by the Urban League revealed that not one manager out of ten interviewed in the First Hill section of Seattle would rent to a qualified nonwhite applicant, whether Negro, Japanese, Chinese, Filipino or American Indian. In Pasco and Kennewick, the bars against Negroes have been so rigid as to be reminiscent of the Deep South. Middle-class housing is almost completely closed to Negroes in Spokane and they are relegated to the inferior, rundown neighborhoods. The housing picture in Tacoma for minority groups has been described as grim and segregated. Four areas in Seattle that have traditionally prevented Jewish home-ownership—Broadmoor, Highlands, Sand Point Country Club and Windmere—have apparently been joined by Mercerwood, Brydel Wood and Canterbury in maintaining religious discrimination.

The City of Seattle has recently shown a definite interest in commencing an open-occupancy policy in the administration of its urban renewal program. Racially integrated housing is a declared goal, but the membership of the Greater Seattle Housing Council is by no means unanimous in this opinion.

PUBLIC ACCOMMODATIONS

Discrimination, including segregation, is prohibited in a long list of places of "public resort, accommodation, assemblage or amusement" in the State of Washington. A recent bill would add nonsectarian cemeteries, if passed. As in the other civil rights areas, the state laws of Washington are often in advance of public practice.

INTERRACIAL MARRIAGE

There is no Washington law banning interracial marriage.

WEST VIRGINIA

"I wish to conclude by saying that in the implementation of these poli-cies of legal compliance, we will be many years in effecting integration in the true sense of the word, although desegregation may, within itself, come with comparative ease. Our problems exist in the minds of men and we do not feel it is the prerogative of the school administration, or even the courts, to force this change. We do feel, however, obligated not to retard the orderly processes by which men examine and re-ex-amine their attitudes and beliefs to the end that we might devise more effective patterns of human relations and intergroup action. Such is the spirit of democracy."

DR. REX SMITH,
ASSISTANT STATE SUPERINTENDENT OF SCHOOLS IN WEST VIRGINIA

By the fall of 1960 the educational system of West Virginia was completely integrated. From the very moment of its announcement, the official state position was compliance with the Supreme Court decision. In September, 1954, Negro pupils in 22 counties entered formerly all-white schools. One half of the school districts that had maintained segregated schools made moves toward desegregation in that school year. All of the state's white colleges opened their doors to Negro students.

In 1954, the Negro population constituted 5.7% of West Vir-ginia's total. With most of the Negroes concentrated in the southern and eastern counties, desegregation difficulties arose mainly there. Picketing and disturbances occurred in three of the newly desegre-gated communities but only in one, Greenbrier County, did the local school board reverse its desegregation decision. In Boone County, the School Superintendent quelled the first outbreak by seeking and receiving the aid of the student council of the desegregated school. In Marion County, mothers and a few fathers picketed a desegre-gated school for two days. A local judge, issuing an injunction

against them, declared: "If necessary, I'll fill the jail until their feet
are sticking out the window." Peace returned to Marion County.

VOTING

Discrimination in voting is practically unknown in West Virginia.
Negroes are permitted to register freely and to exercise their voting
rights without restriction.

EDUCATION

As mentioned above, the West Virginia public school system was
completely desegregated in all grades from kindergarten to university by 1960. Interestingly, by 1959–60, West Virginia State
College, which prior to 1954 was an all-Negro school, increased
its enrollment of white students to 55%. It would appear that white
students of lower academic qualifications profited the most from
desegregation by finding acceptance in formerly all-Negro colleges
with lower standards. Negroes were not as readily admitted to formerly all-white colleges.

EMPLOYMENT

Discrimination in West Virginia employment is pronounced. No
move toward the promulgation of an FEPC law has yet been made.
Negroes with college degrees are limited to much the same type of
menial jobs as their less-educated fellows. Despite the fact that
West Virginia State College graduates numerous chemical engineers
every year, only one such graduate is currently employed in this
capacity in the Kanawha Valley's large chemical industry. A recent
sign of change was the introduction of a bill in the legislature pro-
posing the creation of a Human Rights Commission with power to
receive and investigate complaints involving racial, religious or
ethnic discrimination. The commission, however, would only have
conciliation power.

HOUSING

Discrimination in access to housing is West Virginia's most pressing discriminatory issue. Substandard housing is not only the problem of minority groups in this state but also of all low-income citizens. Hardly any of the new housing is available to Negroes. In the entire county of Kanawha, less than 100 houses were built for Negroes since 1940. Discrimination is of a total pattern with real estate brokers, property managers and subdivision developers all acting in concert to keep Negroes out of "decent" white neighborhoods. Only Wheeling and Charleston have attempted to find some solution to the dilemma. The Charleston Housing Authority operates 834 nonsegregated units, 217 of which are Negro-occupied; the maximum monthly rent is $60 and the minimum $25 (including utilities), and the average amounts to $38. Most Negroes in the state, however, live in old homes in the midst of slums.

Jews meet with discrimination in West Virginia in their efforts to secure summer homes or permanent residences in resort areas.

PUBLIC ACCOMMODATIONS

Some change has been recorded in the desegregation of public places of accommodation in West Virginia, although hotels, motels, restaurants, swimming pools and most other places of public resort are still restricted to whites only. Most hotels in Huntington, Parkersburg, Clarksburg and Wheeling are now accepting Negro guests. Recently the Charleston City Council adopted an ordinance prohibiting discrimination in hotels.

INTERRACIAL MARRIAGE

West Virginia law forbids marriage between white and Negro.

WISCONSIN

"We once owned property from here to Green Bay and farther. The Federal Government originally, through treaty, promised us they would be our protector if we gave them those lands. Now they've broken our treaty and we feel we have money coming from those lands."

FRANCIS LEON, MEMBER OF THE MENOMINEE INDIAN COMMITTEE FOR THE ADVANCEMENT OF THE INDIAN PEOPLE. KENOSHA, WISCONSIN, JULY 14, 1961

"Termination" is the term used to describe the Government's recent policy of ending federal trusteeship over the assets of Indian tribes that are considered capable of handling their own money, property, services and affairs. On April 30, 1961, termination became final for the large Menominee tribe which inhabits the 234,000-acre Menominee Reservation in Wisconsin.

The Menominees are now being given control of their own affairs after a century of federal guardianship. The sudden transition has brought uncalculated hardship to the tribe. The State of Wisconsin has certainly aggravated the Menominee crisis by refusing to have anything to do with the dispute, contending it is purely a federal matter.

VOTING

Many minority citizens have migrated recently into Wisconsin from the South. Often uninformed as to their state rights and responsibilities, they have not registered to vote. There is, however, no discrimination in Wisconsin voting rights.

EDUCATION

Wisconsin schools appear to be fully integrated on all levels. Since July, 1949, the state has had a statute forbidding racial discrimination or segregation in public schools.

EMPLOYMENT

As early as 1945, Wisconsin enacted an FEPC law. It was, however, devoid of any legal enforcement powers. In 1957 this statute was amended to give the Wisconsin Industrial Commission the power to issue cease-and-desist orders.

About 95% of all the charges brought before the commission have referred to discrimination because of race or color. There is corroborating evidence of considerable bias against the hiring of Negroes, especially in skilled and white-collar positions. Negroes are excluded from participation in many union training programs and management-sponsored apprenticeships.

HOUSING

Resistance to the movement of Negroes and other minority groups into all-white neighborhoods has not been a major problem in Wisconsin. However, urban renewal programs in Milwaukee and other cities which require the condemnation of land and relocation of occupants, threaten to disturb this present harmony. In order to forestall such developments, Governor Nelson, in his 1961 message to the legislature, urged legislation to establish equal opportunity in housing and to strengthen the state's public accommodation laws. He asked that the Governor's Commission on Human Rights be given enforcement jurisdiction over such discrimination. As a result of the governor's prompting, a bill is now pending that would prohibit persons engaged in real estate—including financing agencies—from discriminating in the sale, lease, rental or financing of real estate property.

PUBLIC ACCOMMODATIONS

Wisconsin's existing ban on discrimination in places of public accommodation is to be fortified by the provision for criminal sanctions and imprisonment when a proposed amendment comes into effect.

In March, 1959, the State Board of Regents barred the University of Wisconsin athletic teams from playing in localities where minority team members might be subject to discrimination.

INTERRACIAL MARRIAGE

Wisconsin has no law banning interracial marriage.

WYOMING

"The last frontier, like earlier frontiers, was thoroughly democratic. Most of the new communities adopted some form of woman suffrage— Wyoming had led the way as early as 1869 . . . Democracy was most apparent, however, in social rather than political relationships. Anyone who dressed better than his neighbors, who put on airs, who flaunted domestic help, was looked upon with suspicion. All children went to public schools and the more ambitious of the young men and women to near-by denominational and normal colleges that were early provided by every Western commonwealth. Many races mingled in these frontier communities—British, Germans, Norwegians, Bohemians, a sprinkling of Jews, along with native Americans from bordering states; and there was universal toleration for differences of race, language, and creed. In many respects this last frontier was the most democratic and the most American of all frontiers."

ALLEN NEVINS AND HENRY STEELE COMMAGER,
History of the United States

The casual, inherent democratic tradition remains very strong in Wyoming even today. The state has only a small number of Negro citizens but its discrimination toward them and the Indians, who constitute a more significant minority, is conceded to be less encompassing in practice than that of its bordering neighbors.

VOTING

Wyoming does not restrict the right of any of its citizens to vote. Some difficulties have been encountered in efforts to induce the Indians to use this privilege.

EDUCATION

Owing to the fact that Wyoming has only small communities, of which the cities of Cheyenne and Casper with approximately 40,-000 each are the two largest, segregation is practically nonexistent in the public education system of the state. Segregated housing patterns have not resulted in segregated schools in Wyoming and school districts are fairly established in such a way as to cut across the boundaries of the segregated neighborhoods.

EMPLOYMENT

Wyoming has no FEPC law. At present the lack of relevant studies of employment discrimination in the state makes any firm conclusions in this area premature.

HOUSING

Wyoming has never officially espoused segregation as a state policy. Zoning ordinances are said to be based upon the use of property rather than on any distinctions of race, religion or national origin. Several *de facto* segregated areas indisputably exist in the state, however, in which minority groups are living in substandard housing.

The Wyoming State Advisory Committee to the U.S. Commission on Civil Rights has not received any evidence of discrimination in home financing. There is a lack of data on the actual incidence of slum conditions and housing availability to Negroes, Mexican-

Americans, and Indians. In some instances, restrictive covenants are silently enforced to keep "undesirable" minority groups out of white sections. No antidiscriminatory legislation has been proposed in Wyoming.

PUBLIC ACCOMMODATIONS

Discrimination against members of the various minority groups in the use of public facilities appears to be a reality in Wyoming. In February of 1961 a bill was signed into law by Governor Joseph J. Hickey that prohibited discrimination "in all places or agencies which are public in nature or which invite the patronage of the public."

INTERRACIAL MARRIAGE

Wyoming laws prohibit marriage between white and Negro, Malayan or Mongolian.